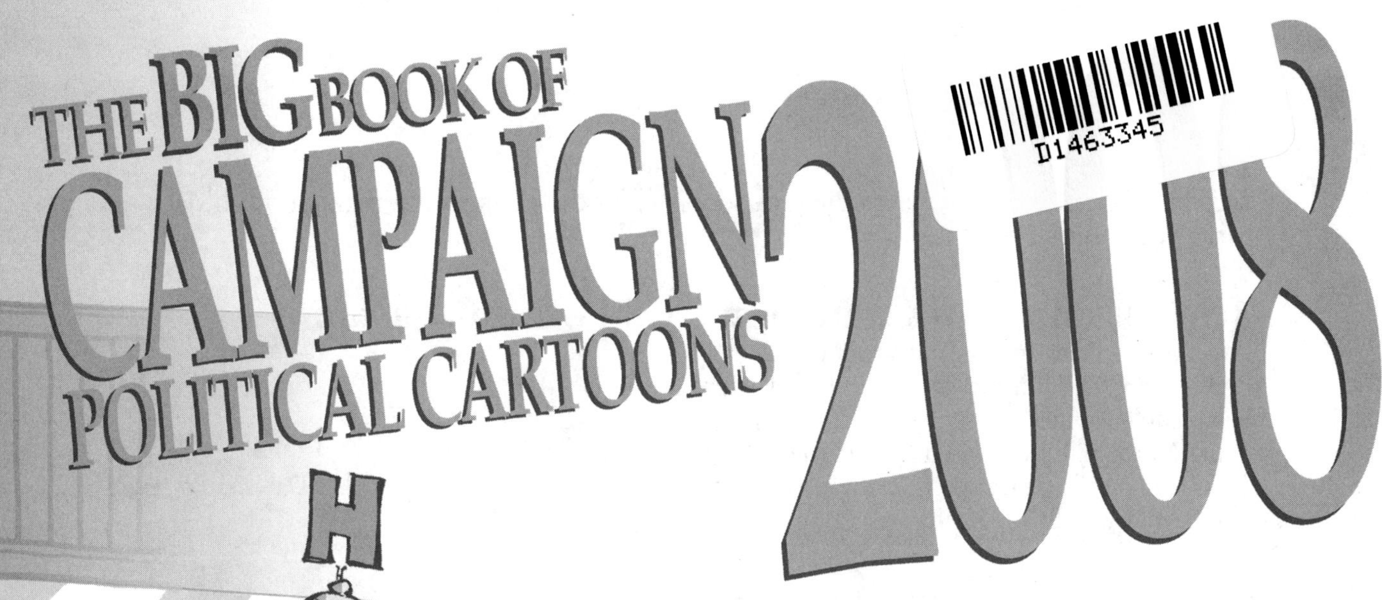

Edited by
Daryl Cagle and
Brian Fairrington

Dedication

This book is dedicated to our brilliant cartoonists, for their support in making our little cartoon business possible.

The BIG Book of Campaign 2008 Political Cartoons

Daryl Cagle, Cartoonist-Editor, Front Cover
Brian Fairrington, Cartoonist-Editor, Back Cover
Susie Cagle, Writer
Laura Norman, Executive Editor for Que Publishing
Thanks to our Cagle Cartoons staff for their contributions: Stacey Fairrington, Cari Dawson Bartley, Bob Bartley and Brian Davis.

International Standard Book Number: 0-7897-3809-0
Library of Congress Cataloging-in-Publication data is on file
Printed in the United States of America
First Printing: September 2008

Bulk Sales.
Que Publishing offers excellent discounts on this book when ordered in quantity for bulk purchases or special sales. For more information, please contact:
U.S. Corporate and Government Sales
1-800-382-3419
corpsales@pearsontechgroup.com

For sales outside the United States, please contact
International Sales
international@pearsoned.com

THE BIG BOOK OF CAMPAIGN POLITICAL CARTOONS 2008

EDITED BY DARYL CAGLE & BRIAN FAIRRINGTON

Table of Contents

About this book

The 2008 presidential campaign was the longest ever, and was a marathon for America's political cartoonists. This year our files were overflowing with cartoons for our annual "Best Political Cartoons" book and we had to do a second book just about the campaign.

This book is a history of the campaign, told in cartoons. We started out with Hillary Clinton and Rudy Giuliani as the frontrunners. Barack Obama and John McCain were once long shots; at one point, the pundits and cartoonists had totally written McCain off as a lost cause – and it's still not over yet. We're closing the book at the time of the conventions so it will be in bookstores at least a month before election day – right after Obama chose Joe Biden as his running mate, and after John Edwards' affair was revealed (we had to get that in). As I write this, I don't know who will win, and the suspense is killing me!

We focused on the most popular, most widely syndicated cartoonists for this collection of Campaign '08 cartoons. Each cartoonist in this book is syndicated to close to 900 newspapers and magazines around the world, and they present a wide range of styles and viewpoints. All the cartoonists here can be seen on our site at www.cagle.com and our online store at www.politicalcartoons.com. Come! Visit us online!

TAYLOR JONES
Politicalcartoons.com

Taylor Jones
2008

About the Editor-Cartoonists

Daryl Cagle

Daryl is the daily editorial cartoonist for MSNBC.com. Daryl's editorial cartoon site with MSNBC.com (www.cagle.com) is the most popular cartoon website of any kind on the Internet. It is also the most widely used education site in social studies classrooms around the world.

For the past 30 years, Daryl has been one of America's most prolific cartoonists. Raised in California, Daryl went to college at UC Santa Barbara and then moved to New York City, where he worked for 10 years with Jim Henson's Muppets, illustrating scores of books, magazines, calendars, and all manner of products.

In 2001, Daryl started a new syndicate, Cagle Cartoons, Inc. (www.caglecartoons.com), which distributes the cartoons of 50 editorial cartoonists and columnists to more than 800 newspapers in the United States, Canada, and Latin America. Daryl is a past president of the National Cartoonists Society and current president of the National Cartoonists Society Foundation. He is a frequent guest on Fox News, CNN and MSNBC. Daryl is a popular and entertaining public speaker. Interested in having Daryl speak to your group? Contact us through www.caglecartoons.com for more information.

Daryl Cagle and Brian Fairrington by Brian Fairrington

Brian Fairrington

A graduate of Arizona State University, Brian earned a bachelor's degree in political science and a master's degree in communications.

Brian is one of the most accomplished young cartoonists in the country. Brian was the recipient of the Locher Award, the Charles M. Schulz Award, and several Society of Professional Journalists awards and Gold Circle Awards. He is a regular on the Phoenix-based television talk show Horizon, for which one of his appearances garnered an Emmy award. Brian has also been a guest on Imus inthe Morning and was recently featured on CBS News Sunday Morning.

Brian's cartoons are nationally syndicated to more than 800 newspapers and publications in America with Caglecartoons.com. His cartoons have appeared in The New York Times, USA Today, and Time, as well as on CNN, MSNBC, and Fox News. Additionally, his cartoons regularly appear on www.cagle.msnbc.com.

Brian is a native of Arizona and is married to the wonderful Stacey Heywood and they have four children.

We Want to Hear From You

As the reader of this book, you are our most important critic and commentator. We value your opinion and want to know what we're doing right, what we could do better, what areas you'd like to see us publish in, and any other words of wisdom you're willing to pass our way.

As an associate publisher for Que Publishing, I welcome your comments. You can email or write me directly to let me know what you did or didn't like about this book—as well as what we can do to make our books better.

Please note that I cannot help you with technical problems related to the topic of this book. We do have a User Services group, however, where I will forward specific technical questions related to the book.

When you write, please be sure to include this book's title and author as well as your name, email address, and phone number. I will carefully review your comments and share them with the author and editors who worked on the book.

Email: feedback@quepublishing.com
Mail: Greg Wiegand
Associate Publisher
Que Publishing
800 East 96th Street
Indianapolis, IN
46240 USA

Our Wonderful Publisher
by Brian Fairrington

How to Draw Hillary

But of course with all this excitement, a Barack-lash was inevitable. As Obama made more policy decisions pandering to conservatives, he lost a grip on his liberal base and earned the familiar "flip-flopper" name, along with some scathing under-his-breath criticisms from former ally Jesse Jackson.

As a cartoon character, Hillary was definitely the best choice for president, and her dive in the polls was a disappointment for political cartoonists.

I don't make up my own cartoon characters; the world provides me with characters. Great characters. Better characters than I could ever make up. I sit around at my desk all day, watching Fox News and MSNBC. I get angry and I think of cartoons. It's the good life. Compared to a comic strip cartoonist, I've got it easy. Comic strip artists spend their whole

careers developing characters in tiny, daily increments. It takes years and years of strips before readers know just what is in Lucy's mind when she holds the football for Charlie Brown that kind of intimate knowledge of character gives cartoons wonderful depth. When our readers know our characters, we can draw cartoons that are rewarding just because we see the character acting as we already know he will. A subtle bit of body language can be a punch line when readers really know the characters, and it is the best kind of humor when the gag was years in the making.

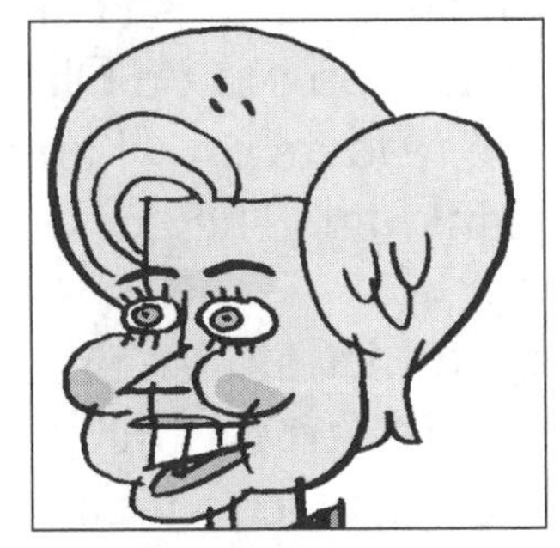

Hillary Clinton is a cartoon character that has taken many years to develop, and every editorial cartoonist can claim her as his own. We know Bill Clinton as intimately as we know Charlie Brown. We know Hillary as intimately as we know Lucy. They are an editorial cartoonist's treasure.

I drew a cartoon with Bill and Hillary that was probably my most reprinted, most popular cartoon ever. They were on a book tour, and I drew Bill and Hillary at a table together, signing books. Bill had his book open with a Playboy style foldout dropping out of the book, and Hillary whacked Bill on the side of his head with her book. There were no words, just facial expressions and body language. My readers loved it! Oh! The mail I got on that one!

As Hillary's campaign prospects faded, I was seeing my best characters fade away. Obama is easy to draw, but there's noth-

ing behind the long face no pain we all shared, no national embarrassment, no anger, no crazy, complex, cheating spouse. For all the excitement of his supporters, Obama is dull. He's a straight man, commenting on the events around him, or riding the crest of a wave, or driving a steamroller over Hillary. There isn't any facial expression I can put on Obama that will make the readers say, "I know just what he's thinking!" The guy is a cartoon disaster.

John McCain isn't much better. The term of art for McCain is "pudding-face." In fact, McCain is more like tapioca, with a lumpy face that looks like he has his cheeks filled with marbles; that doesn't help me much. McCain has a reputation for a hot temper, which is fun for a cartoonist, but we haven't seen enough of his temper to expect it in a cartoon. Al Gore and John Kerry were stiff, dull, and just as bad for cartoonists.

When President Bush ran against Sen. Kerry in 2004, there was no doubt that the best choice for the cartooning business was Bush. In the past eight years we've had great material for cartoons. We've had wars, terrorist attacks, and some ugly times in Washington, but there have been some great cartoons during the Bush administration. Tough times make for good cartoons, too. In fact, I'll bet my cartoons would look better if I knocked my head against the wall a few times.

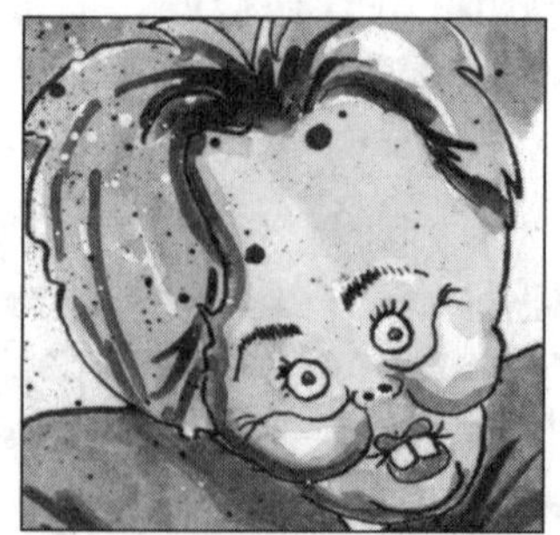

Daryl Cagle

Why the New Yorker's Obama Cover was a LOUSY Cartoon, by Daryl Cagle

In July of 2008, cable news channels and bloggers were buzzing about the New Yorker magazine cover featuring Barack Obama dressed in Muslim garb, and Michelle Obama with an afro and machine gun, doing a "terrorist fist bump" in the Oval Office while an American flag burns in the fireplace. The cartoon by Barry Blitt drew immediate condemnation from the Obama and McCain camps.

In an interview on the Huffington Post website, New Yorker editor David Remnick argues, "Obviously I wouldn't have run a cover just to get attention I ran the cover because I thought it had something to say. What I think it does is hold up a mirror to the prejudice and dark imaginings about both Obamas it combines a number of images that have been propagated, not by everyone on the right but by some, about Obama's supposed 'lack of patriotism' or his being 'soft on terrorism' or the idiotic notion that somehow Michelle Obama is the second coming of the Weathermen or most violent Black Panthers. That somehow all this is going to come to the Oval Office.

"The idea that we would publish a cover saying these things literally, I think, is just not in the vocabulary of what we do and who we are, we've run many, many satirical political covers. Ask the Bush administration how many."

Cartoonist Barry Blitt defends the cover by saying, "It seemed to me that depicting the concept would show it as the fear-mongering ridiculousness that it is." So the cover cartoon is simply an exaggeration of the allegations against the Obamas.

There are rules to political cartoons that allow cartoonists to draw in an elegant, simple shorthand that readers understand. Exaggeration is a well-worn tool of political cartoonists; we use it all the time. I've drawn President Bush as the King of England, to exaggerate his autocratic tendencies. I've drawn the president as a dog, peeing all over the globe to mark his territory. I exaggerate every day, and I don't expect my readers to take my exaggerations seriously but when I draw an absurdly exaggerated political cartoon, I'm looking for some truth to exaggerate to make my point. A typical stand-up comedian will tell jokes about things the audience already knows or agrees with "it's funny because it's true," or true as the comedian sees it. It is the same for cartoonists. Our readers know that we're exaggerating to make a point we believe in.

Cartoonists have a great advantage over journalists in that we can draw whatever we want. We can put words into the mouths of politicians that the politicians never said. Cartoons can be outrageous in their exaggeration; we draw things that never happened, and never could happen but we have a contract with the readers who understand that we're drawing crazy things that convey our own views. The New Yorker's Obama cover fails to keep that contract with readers. Cartoonists don't exaggerate anything just because we have the freedom to do so; we exaggerate to communicate in a way that our readers understand.

There is no frame of reference in The New Yorker's cover to put the scene into perspective. Following the rules of political cartoons, I could fix it. I would have Obama think in a thought balloon, "I must be in the nightmare of some conservative." With that, the scene is shown to be in the mind of someone the cartoonist disagrees with and we have defined the target of the cartoon as crazy conservatives with their crazy dreams.

Since readers expect cartoonists to convey some truth as we see it, depicting someone else's point of view in a cartoon has to be shown to be someone else's point of view, otherwise it is reasonable for readers to see the cartoon as somehow being the cartoonist's point of view, no matter how absurd the cartoon is. That is where The New Yorker's cover cartoon fails.

I reserve the right to be as offensive as I want in my cartoons, and to exaggerate however I please -- but I want my cartoons to work, to be good cartoons. A cartoon that fails to communicate its message in a way that readers understand is nothing more than a bad cartoon.

- Daryl Cagle

The New Yorker cover by Barry Blitt

New Yorker Cover

There was one election cartoon this year that really whipped everyone into a frenzy. The New Yorker cover satirically depicting Barack Obama and his wife Michelle as radical Islamic militants didn't just offend the Democrats – Republicans were up in arms, too (perhaps if only for the opportunity to attack the venerably liberal New Yorker). Few people spoke to the incredible irony of American leaders condemning an act of free speech. Luckily, from one harmless but crappy cartoon were born many wittier ones.

STEPHANE PERAY
Thailand

DARYL CAGLE
MSNBC.COM

JIMMY MARGULIES
The Record (NJ)

CAMERON CARDOW, Ottawa Citizen (Canada)

JOHN DARKOW
Columbia Daily
Tribune (MO)

NEW YORKER COVER

JOHN COLE
Scranton Times-Tribune

DARYL CAGLE
MSNBC.COM

WHAT A FUNNY MAGAZINE COVER. NO ONE COULD BELIEVE THIS.

HA. HA.

WE'RE ALL GONNA DIE!

THE NEW YORKER

DARYL CAGLE MSNBC.com

KNOW THE DIFFERENCE:

JOHN COLE
Scranton Times-Tribune

SATIRE.

SARCASM.

MALICIOUS SLANDER

SOPHISTICATED SATIRE

R.J. MATSON
St. Louis Post Dispatch

©MATSON
ST. LOUIS POST-DISPATCH
caglecartoons.com

OSMANI SIMANCA
Brazil

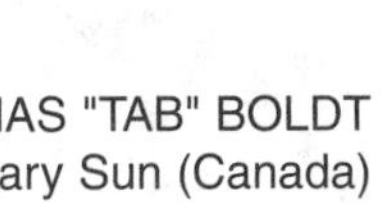

THOMAS "TAB" BOLDT
Calgary Sun (Canada)

PAT BAGLEY, Salt Lake Tribune (UT)

MIKE LANE
Cagle Cartoons

BOB ENGLEHART
Hartford Courant

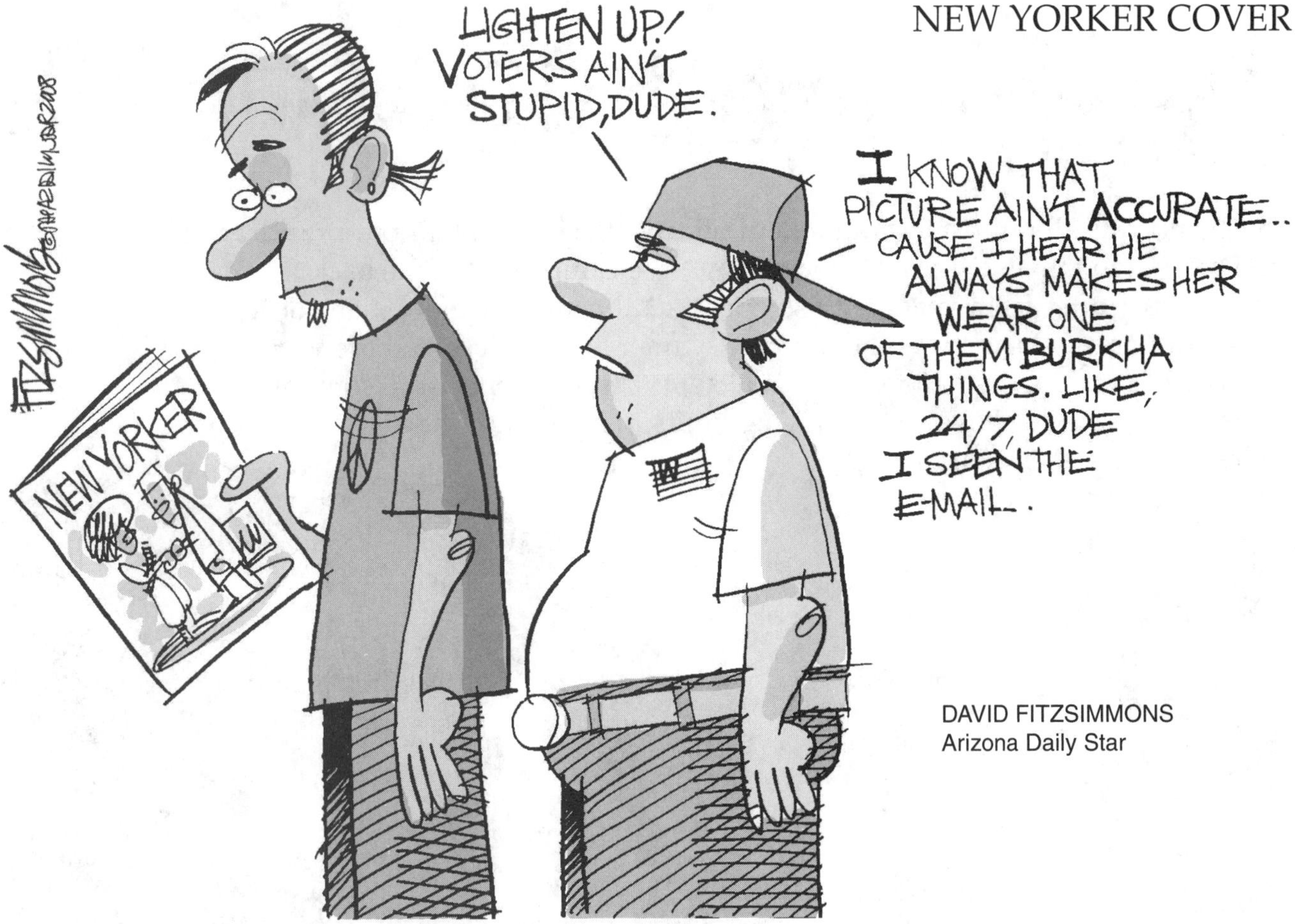

LIGHTEN UP! VOTERS AIN'T STUPID, DUDE.

I KNOW THAT PICTURE AIN'T ACCURATE.. CAUSE I HEAR HE ALWAYS MAKES HER WEAR ONE OF THEM BURKHA THINGS. LIKE, 24/7, DUDE I SEEN THE E-MAIL.

DAVID FITZSIMMONS
Arizona Daily Star

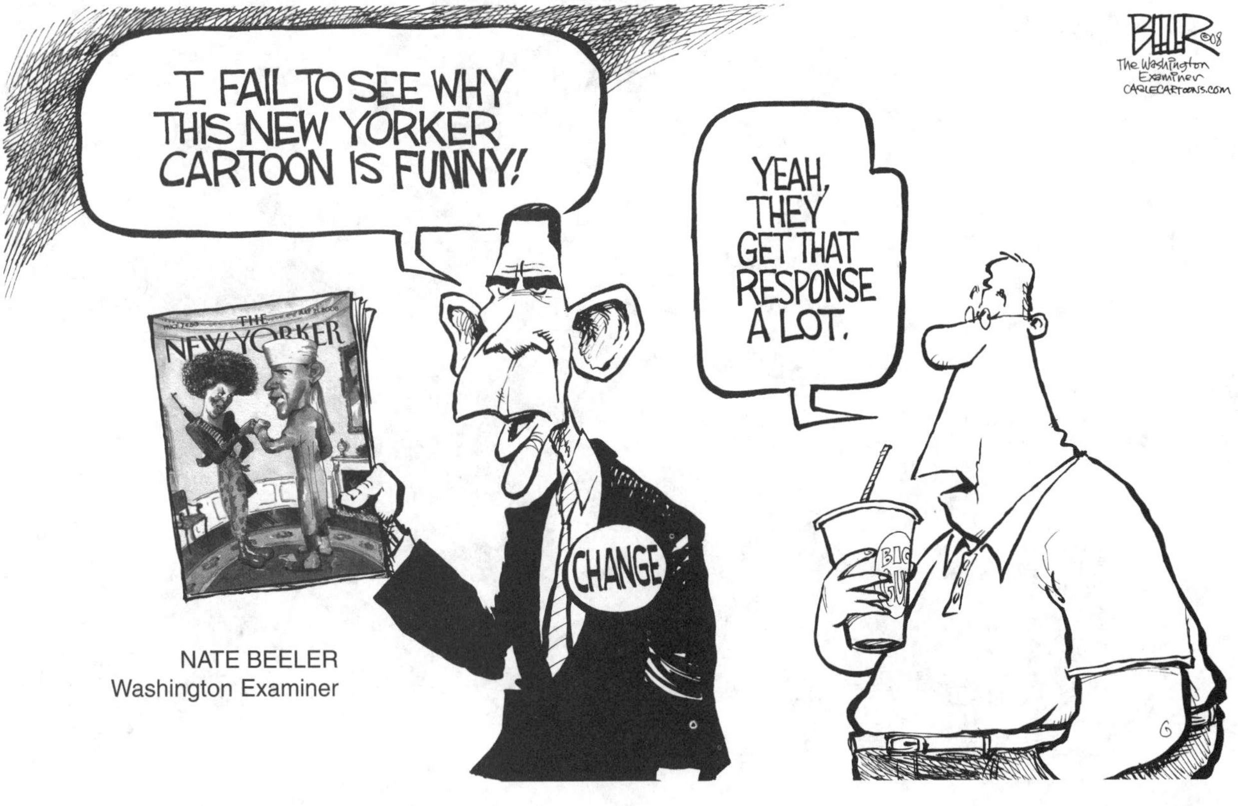

I FAIL TO SEE WHY THIS NEW YORKER CARTOON IS FUNNY!

YEAH, THEY GET THAT RESPONSE A LOT.

CHANGE

NATE BEELER
Washington Examiner

Campaign Fundraising

The Democrats all-out trounced the Republicans this year in that pre-presidential mad cash-grab they like to call "fundraising"; the campaign to take back the White House after eight years of Bush energized liberals far more than conservatives. But Barack Obama was the ultimate winner, having received the vast majority of his donations from individual supporters in contrast to companies or organizations, which have stricter giving limits, while Hillary pumped her own funds into her failing campaign.

JOHN COLE
Scranton Times-Tribune

CLINTON
$
FUNDRAISING
HSU
© MATSON
ST. LOUIS POST-DISPATCH
caglecartoons.com

"ONE BAD BUNDLE DOESN'T SPOIL THE WHOLE BUNCH!"

R.J. MATSON, St. Louis Post Dispatch

R.J. MATSON
Roll Call

BOB ENGLEHART
Hartford Courant

TAYLOR JONES
Politicalcartoons.com

JIMMY MARGULIES, The Record (NJ)

JOHN COLE
Scranton Times-Tribune

MICHAEL MCPARLANE
Politicalcartoons.com

JIMMY MARGULIES
The Record (NJ)

JOHN COLE
Scranton Times-Tribune

M.e. COHEN
Politicalcartoons.com

JIMMY MARGULIES, The Record (NJ)

R.J. MATSON, St. Louis Post Dispatch

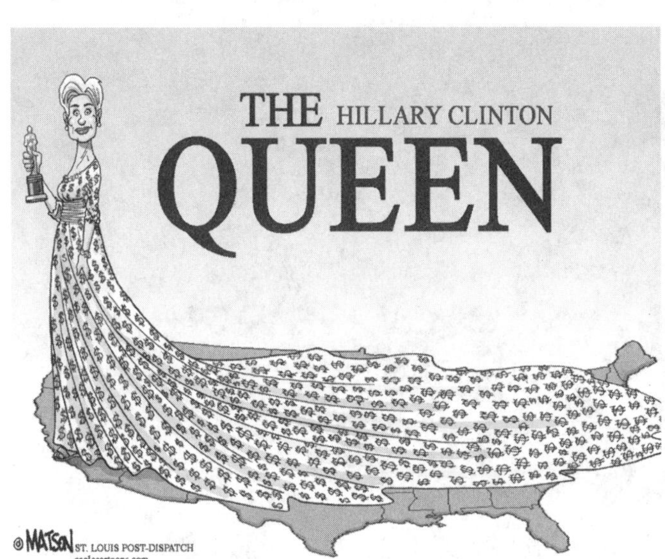

R.J. MATSON
St. Louis Post Dispatch

THE NATURAL

R.J. MATSON
The New York Observer

The Debates!

A special kind of desperation seemed to be fueling the presidential debates this campaign season. Perhaps it was the immensely crowded field of candidates or the results of the bitter cloud that descended over our nation during the Bush administration; but whatever it was, it sure drove some of the candidates, journos, and spectators to extreme measures. Between the many, many yapping candidates, the YouTube debate craziness and harshly worded attacks on their fellow politicos and Obama, the debates were an "undignified" two-party circus perfect for cartoonists.

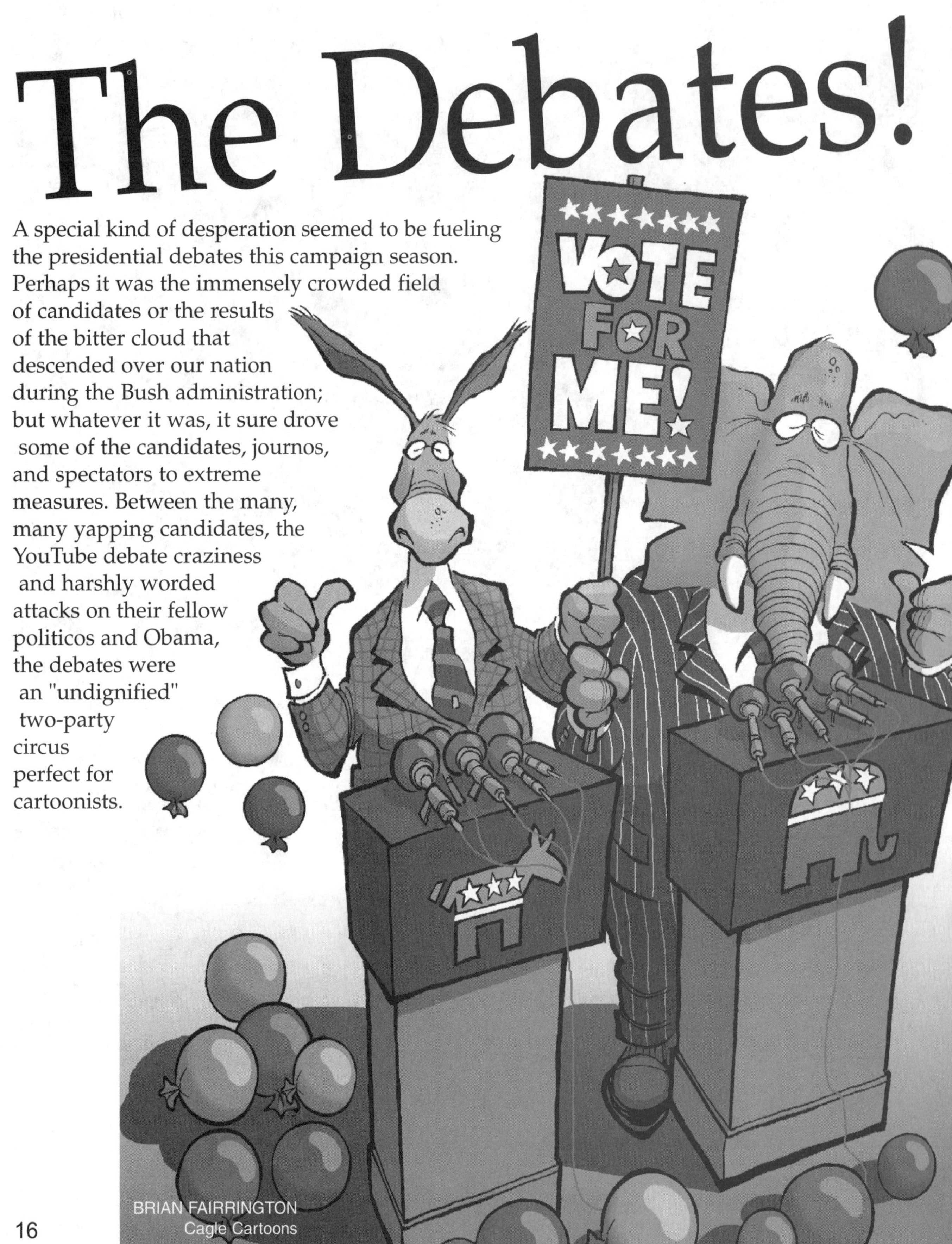

BRIAN FAIRRINGTON
Cagle Cartoons

Turn off that violent video game, so I can watch the Clinton-Obama debate...

This IS the debate...

MORTAL KOMBAT

MARGULIES
©2008 JimMarg@aol.com

JIMMY MARGULIES
The Record (NJ)

JOE HELLER
Green Bay Press Gazette

R.J. MATSON
Roll Call

PAT BAGLEY
Salt Lake Tribune (UT)

JOHN TREVER
Albuquerque Journal

R.J. MATSON
The New York Observer

"AM I THE ONLY ONE THINKING DEBATE FATIGUE HAS SET IN?"

PAT BAGLEY, Salt Lake Tribune (UT)

NATE BEELER, Washington Examiner

R.J. MATSON, New York Observer

Oprah Endorses Obama

Taylor Jones
OPRAH WINFREY
Seal of Approval
I, OPRAH WINFREY, DO SOLEMNLY DECLARE MY SUPPORT FOR BARACK H. OBAMA FOR PRESIDENT IN 2008.
My LEGISLATIVE ACCOMPLISHMENTS:
1.
2.
3.
4.
5.
©Taylor Jones
Politicalcartoons.com

TAYLOR JONES, Politicalcartoons.com

Oprah stepped "out of her pew" and gave Barack Obama a huge boost in his run for the White House when she endorsed the Illinois senator. The move underscored just how powerful a media force the daytime television diva truly is; Oprah was largely credited with broadening Obama's support among women, thus helping him defeat Hillary Clinton in the first influential Iowa primary.

But all was not perfect with the Oprah-Obama campaign. Oprah.com was barraged with hate mail from angry fans who saw Oprah as a traitor to the feminist cause after she not only endorsed Obama, but joined him on a campaign tour of Iowa, New Hampshire, and South Carolina. Luckily for her, the tide quickly shifted from Hillary to Barack, and Oprah was back on the winning team. Or was that tide her doing all along?

JOE HELLER
Green Bay
Press-Gazette

R.J. MATSON, Roll Call

DARYL CAGLE
MSNBC.COM

12/2 DARKOW 2007
COLUMBIA DAILY TRIBUNE
CAGLECARTOONS.COM

Oprah ♥

SHE IS SO INFLUENTIAL, SHE HAS ME CONVINCED!

ME TOO! THAT'S WHY I'M VOTING FOR OPRAH!

JOHN DARKOW, Columbia Daily Tribune (MO

ERIC ALLIE, Politicalcartoons.com

LARRY WRIGHT, Detroit News

If you're concerned about a woman holding the most powerful job in the world... let me assure you...
HILLARY FOR PRESIDENT

OPRAH SAYS: Vote for OBAMA
So am I... SO AM I!
MARGULIES
©2007 JimMarg@aol.com

JIMMY MARGULIES, The Record (NJ)

ROHRSCHACH TEST:
DO YOU SEE...
A) A FUTURE PRESIDENT?
B) A POLITICAL GREENHORN?
C) THE LATEST PRODUCT FROM OPRAH© INC.?
D) THE MULTI-RACIAL SECOND COMING OF JOHN EDWARDS?
E) BARACK WHO?

OBAMABO

JOHN COLE
Scranton Times-Tribune

OPRAH?
mcparlane

MICHAEL MCPARLANE
Politicalcartoons.com

J.D. CROWE, Mobile Register

M.e. COHEN, Politicalcartoons.com

BRIAN FAIRRINGTON
Cagle Cartoons

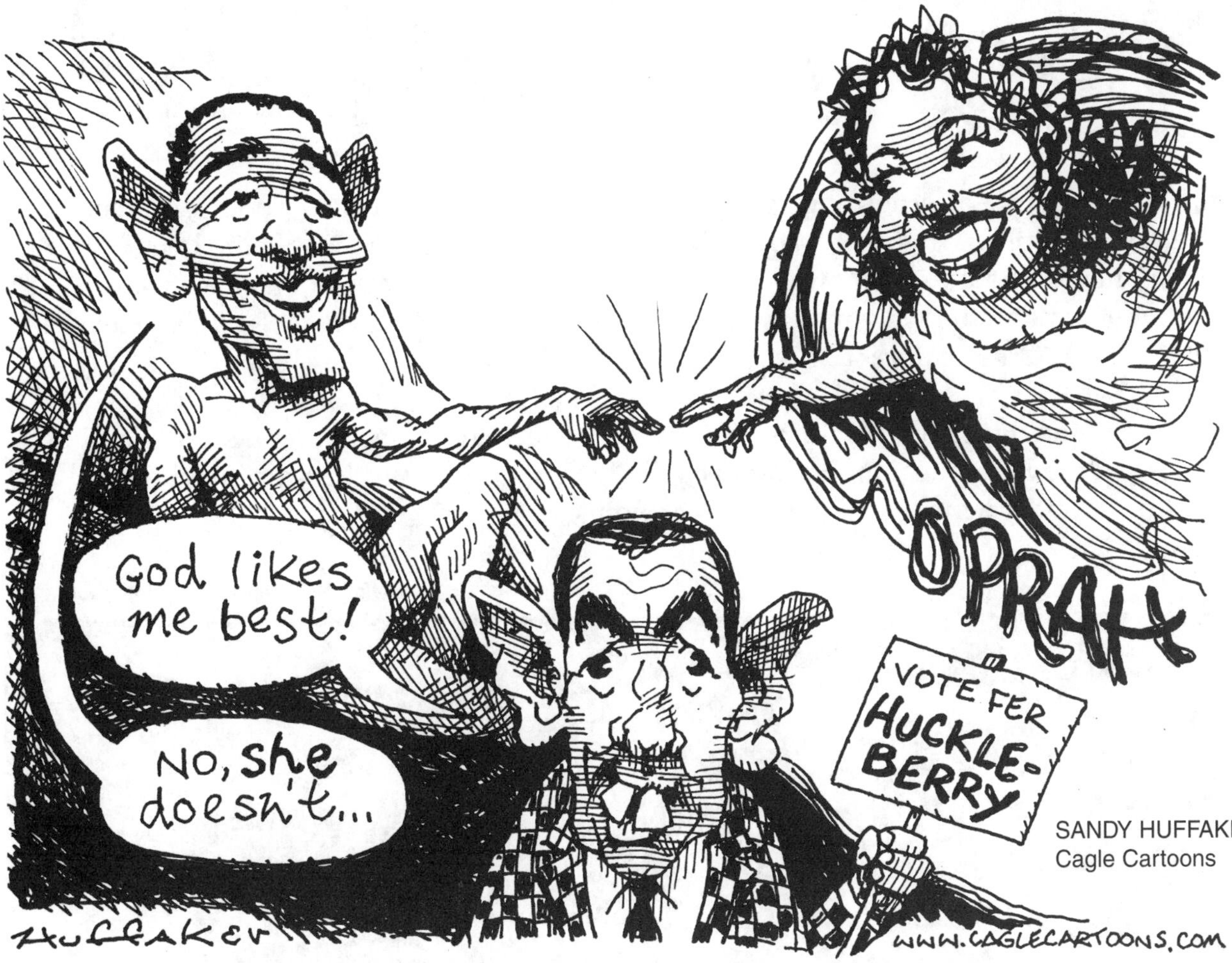

God likes me best!
No, she doesn't...
OPRAH
VOTE FER HUCKLE-BERRY
HUFFAKER
WWW.CAGLECARTOONS.COM

SANDY HUFFAKER
Cagle Cartoons

THAT'S IT....THE GLOVES ARE COMING OFF! GET ME JERRY SPRINGER!!!
OBAMA
OPRAH

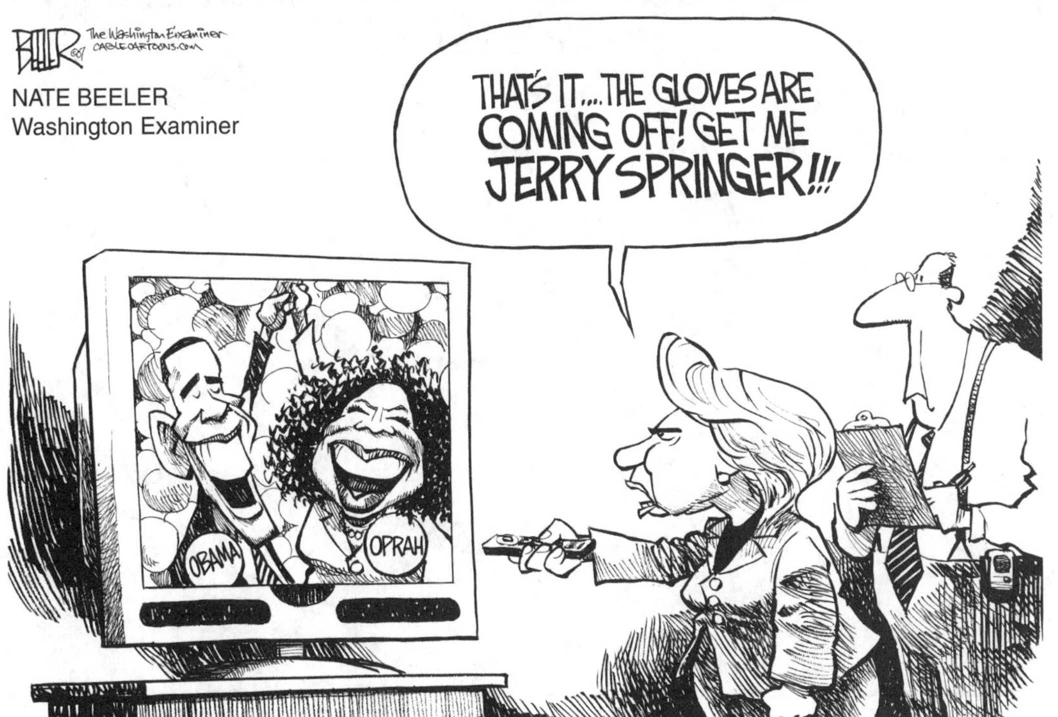

NATE BEELER
Washington Examiner

Fred Thompson

Law and Order district attorney and real-life former Tennessee Sen. Fred Thompson reentered the political sphere this year with a bid for president, though it was short-lived. After announcing his candidacy on an awkward talk-show junket, Thompson made a strong initial showing among the early mass of Republican hopefuls. He even asked to be released from his Law and Order contract.

But all was for naught; Thompson dropped out of the race in January, after a slow slide into fourth place in the Republican polls. Yet between his goofy grin and his trophy wife, Fred Thompson was still a winner in the eyes of cartoonists.

BOB ENGLEHART, Hartford Courant

J.D. CROWE
Mobile Register

NATE BEELER
Washington Examiner

AFTER MUCH QUIET CONTEMPLATION, AH HAVE DECIDED TO WITHDRAW MY CANDIDA—

I'm testing the water...
Taking the pulse...
Gauging the interest...
FRED THOMPSON
FRED THOMPSON
FRED THOMPSON

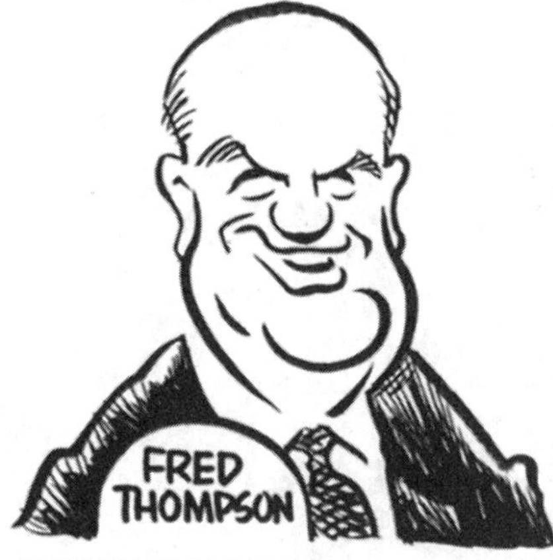

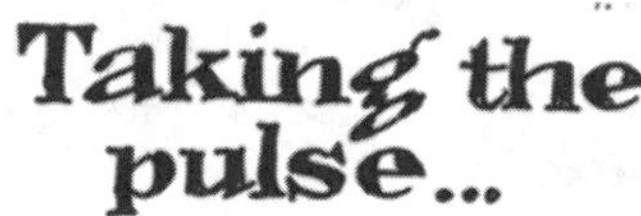

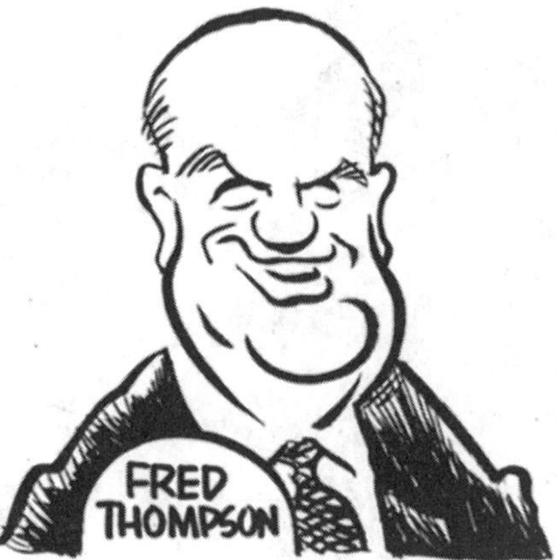

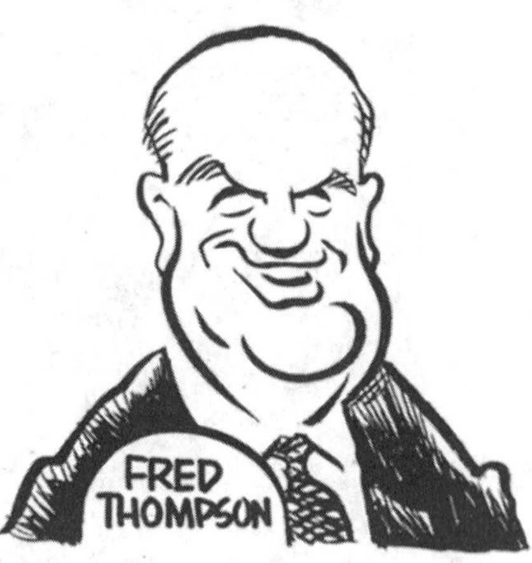

JIMMY MARGULIES, The Record (NJ)

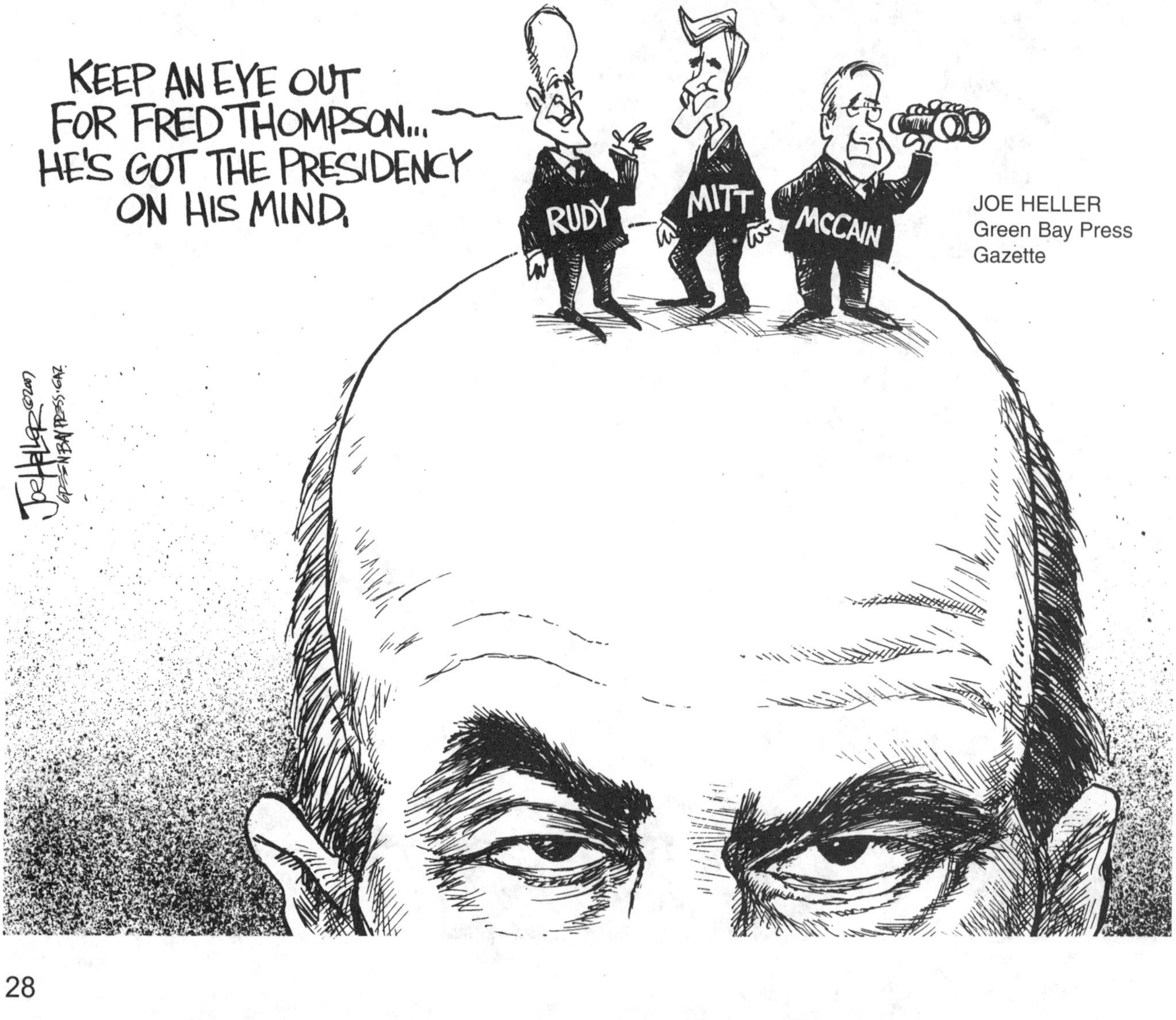

KEEP AN EYE OUT FOR FRED THOMPSON... HE'S GOT THE PRESIDENCY ON HIS MIND.
RUDY
MITT
McCAIN

JOE HELLER
Green Bay Press
Gazette

Listening to the rumblings
MARGULIES
FRED THOMPSON

Calibrating the measure...
FRED THOMPSON

...for my campaign of decisive leadership.
FRED THOMPSON

R.J. MATSON
St. Louis
Post Dispatch

THOMPSON
'08
©MATSON ROLL CALL
caglecartoons.com

"THAT'S A MIGHTY FINE HOLE YOU'VE DUG."

AM I PLAYING A SENATOR, A DISTRICT ATTORNEY OR A PRESIDENTIAL CANDIDATE?
Fred Thompson
caglecartoons.com
courant.com/boblog

BOB ENGLEHART, Hartford Courant

Mike Keefe THE DENVER POST 07/29/07
DON'T RUSH ME. I'M STILL THINKING ABOUT IT.
FRED THOMPSON

MIKE KEEFE, Denver Post

A BRIEF HISTORY OF THE FRED THOMPSON CAMPAIGN
TODAY, I DECLARE MY CANDIDACY FOR PRESIDENT OF THE UNITED STATES.
TODAY, I WITHDRAW MY CANDIDACY FOR PRESIDENT OF THE UNITED STATES.
©MATSON ROLL CALL
caglecartoons.com

R.J. MATSON, Roll Call

Mike Keefe THE DENVER POST 09/09/07 www.caglecartoons.com
MIKE KEEFE
Denver Post
I'M READY FOR MY CLOSE-UP, AMERICA!
FReD
#@*! CAMERA HOG!
GOP

FRED '08
THOMPSON R PRESIDENT

R.J. MATSON
St. Louis Post
Dispatch

WASHINGTON
LOBBYIST

©MATSON
ST. LOUIS POST-DISPATCH
caglecartoons.com

A FRESH FACE FOR THE REPUBLICAN PARTY

I KNOW THE CONSERVATIVES THINK HE'S THE MOST ATTRACTIVE CANDIDATE...
...BUT WE'RE RUNNING OUT OF MAKEUP!
FRED THOMPSON-
a face only a mother COULD LOVE

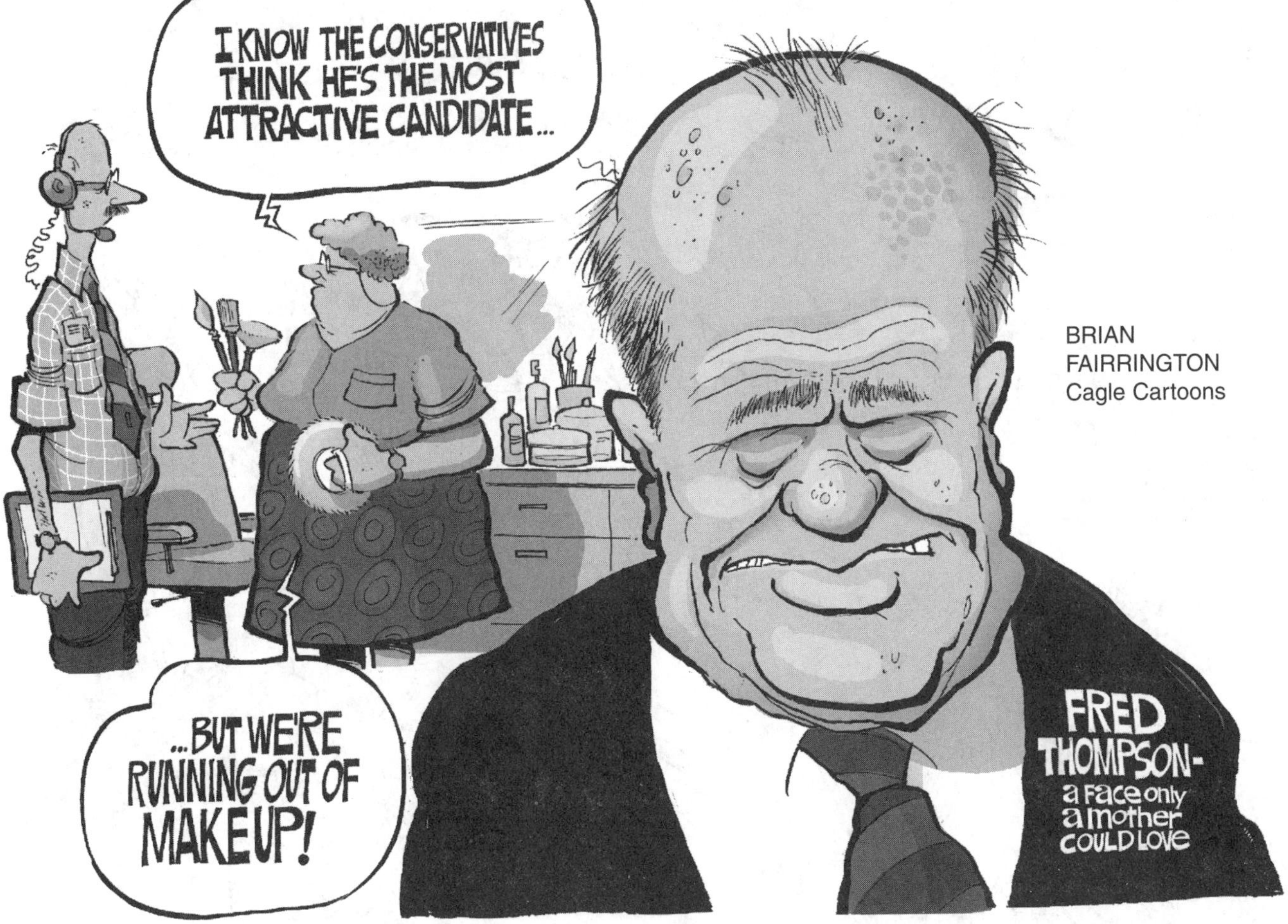

BRIAN
FAIRRINGTON
Cagle Cartoons

WE NEED A FRESH FACE...
GOP PREZ CANDI-DATES

BAGLEY
FRED THOMPSON '08

PAT BAGLEY
Salt Lake Tribune

That boy Thompson's SHIFTLESS!
FRED'S STO
GOP GARAGE
ICE
RC
MOON PIE
Huffaker
www.caglecartoons.com

SANDY HUFFAKER
Cagle Cartoons

SANDY HUFFAKER
Cagle Cartoons

MIKE KEEFE
Denver Post

MARGULIES
©2007 JimMarg@aol.com

I knew Ronald Reagan... Ronald Reagan was a friend of mine... and Fred Thompson, you're no Ronald Reagan...

BONZO

THOMPSON

JIMMY MARGULIES
The Record (NJ)

IF eLeCTeD PReSIDENT I'LL OPPOSe eQUAL RIGHTS FOR WOMeN. eLIMINATe IMPORTANT SOCIAL SeRVICeS. PROMOTe eXPeNSIVe AND WASTeFUL DeFeNSe PROGRAMS WHILe CUTTING eDUCATION PROGRAMS. DO MY BeST TO DeSTROY THe MIDDLe CLASS, AND OH YeAH, IGNORe THe AIDS ePIDeMIC.
THOMPSON
HUFFAKER
WWW.CAGLECARTOONS.COM

SANDY HUFFAKER
Cagle Cartoons

M.e. Cohen
Humorink.com
THeRe, IS THAT ReAGANeSQUe eNOUGH FOR YOU!

M.e. COHEN
Politicalcartoons.com

Crying Hillary

A day before the New Hampshire primary, Hillary Clinton welled up while speaking to voters about balancing her personal and professional lives. Hillary said she cracked under the exhaustion of a grueling campaign schedule, but though she did not technically shed a tear, critics immediately jumped on Hillary for such a blatant (and manipulative?) display of ladylike emotions. But as soon as the cold-hearted media changed their tune and rallied around Hillary's right to cry, the senator seemed to take it as an invitation and began welling up at anything. Cartoonists didn't have much sympathy for Hillary at any point in the melodrama.

PAT BAGLEY
Salt Lake Tribune (UT)

ADAM ZYGLIS
Buffalo News

WEEP! YOU LIED TO ME!
WAAAAAAAAAA! I WANT A CHANGE!
POLL
CRISTO KOMAR

CHRISTO KOMARNITSKI
Bulgaria

Performance Enhancing Substances

Roger Clemens

Hillary Clinton

JIMMY MARGULIES
The Record (NJ)

SANDY HUFFAKER
Cagle Cartoons

SANDY HUFFAKER
Cagle Cartoons

MIKE KEEFE
Denver Post

PETAR PISMESTROVIC
Austria

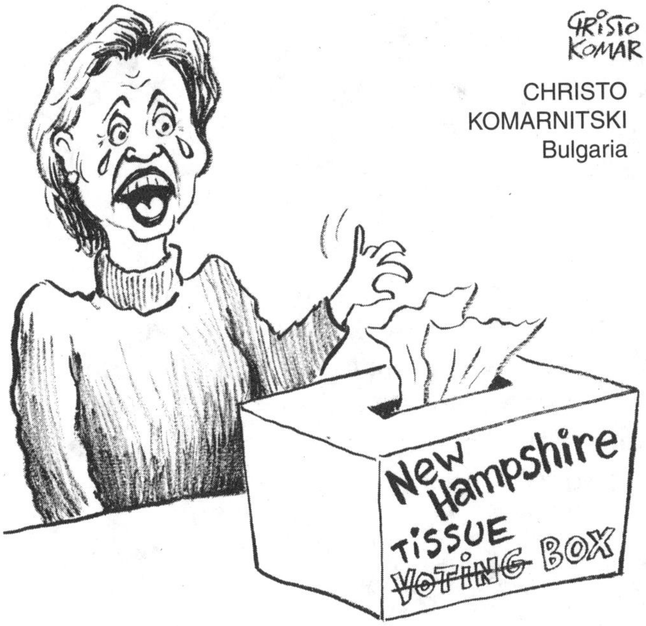

CHRISTO KOMAR
New Hampshire
TISSUE
VOTING BOX

CHRISTO
KOMARNITSKI
Bulgaria

SNIF
Hillary
WILL CRY FOR VOTES

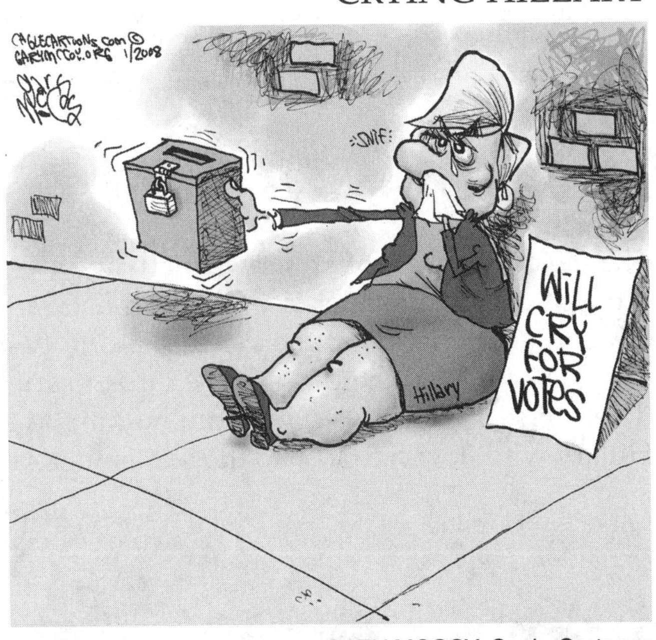

GARY MCCOY, Cagle Cartoons

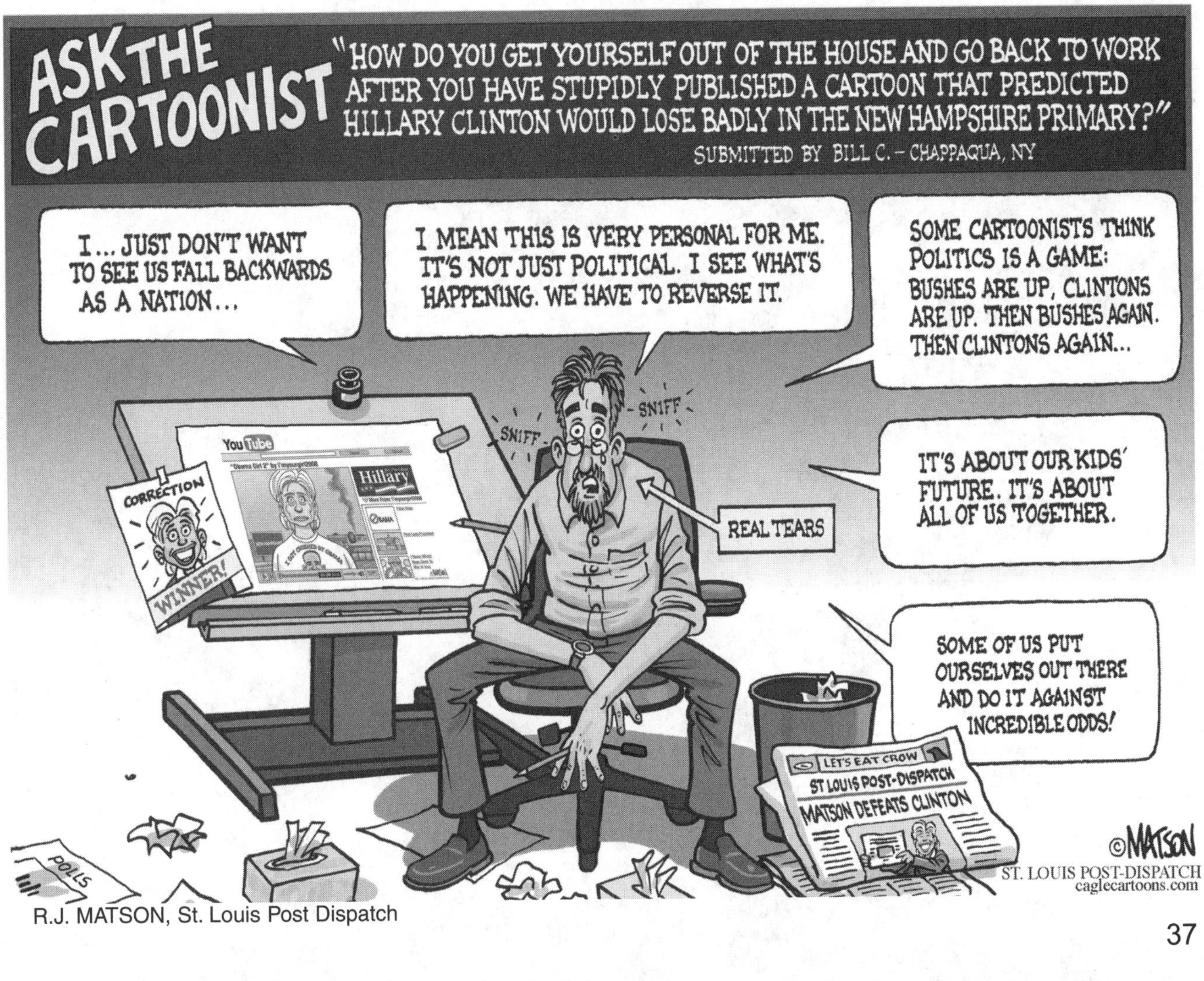

ASK THE CARTOONIST
"HOW DO YOU GET YOURSELF OUT OF THE HOUSE AND GO BACK TO WORK AFTER YOU HAVE STUPIDLY PUBLISHED A CARTOON THAT PREDICTED HILLARY CLINTON WOULD LOSE BADLY IN THE NEW HAMPSHIRE PRIMARY?"
SUBMITTED BY BILL C. – CHAPPAQUA, NY
I... JUST DON'T WANT TO SEE US FALL BACKWARDS AS A NATION...
I MEAN THIS IS VERY PERSONAL FOR ME. IT'S NOT JUST POLITICAL. I SEE WHAT'S HAPPENING. WE HAVE TO REVERSE IT.
SOME CARTOONISTS THINK POLITICS IS A GAME: BUSHES ARE UP, CLINTONS ARE UP. THEN BUSHES AGAIN. THEN CLINTONS AGAIN...
SNIFF
SNIFF
IT'S ABOUT OUR KIDS' FUTURE. IT'S ABOUT ALL OF US TOGETHER.
REAL TEARS
CORRECTION
WINNER!
Hillary
SOME OF US PUT OURSELVES OUT THERE AND DO IT AGAINST INCREDIBLE ODDS!
LET'S EAT CROW
ST LOUIS POST-DISPATCH
MATSON DEFEATS CLINTON
POLLS
©MATSON
ST. LOUIS POST-DISPATCH
caglecartoons.com

R.J. MATSON, St. Louis Post Dispatch

Racial Politics

The historic success of Hillary Clinton and Barack Obama in the Democratic primary brought race and gender issues, which had rarely been at play before in a presidential election, to the center of the debate. And it wasn't just the twittering of the pundits. Both candidates played their respective cards to appeal to voting blocks, and sometimes even to deflect criticism. This certainly did nothing to endear cartoonists to their cause, but it was Hillary who flew too close to the sun on her race-card wings.

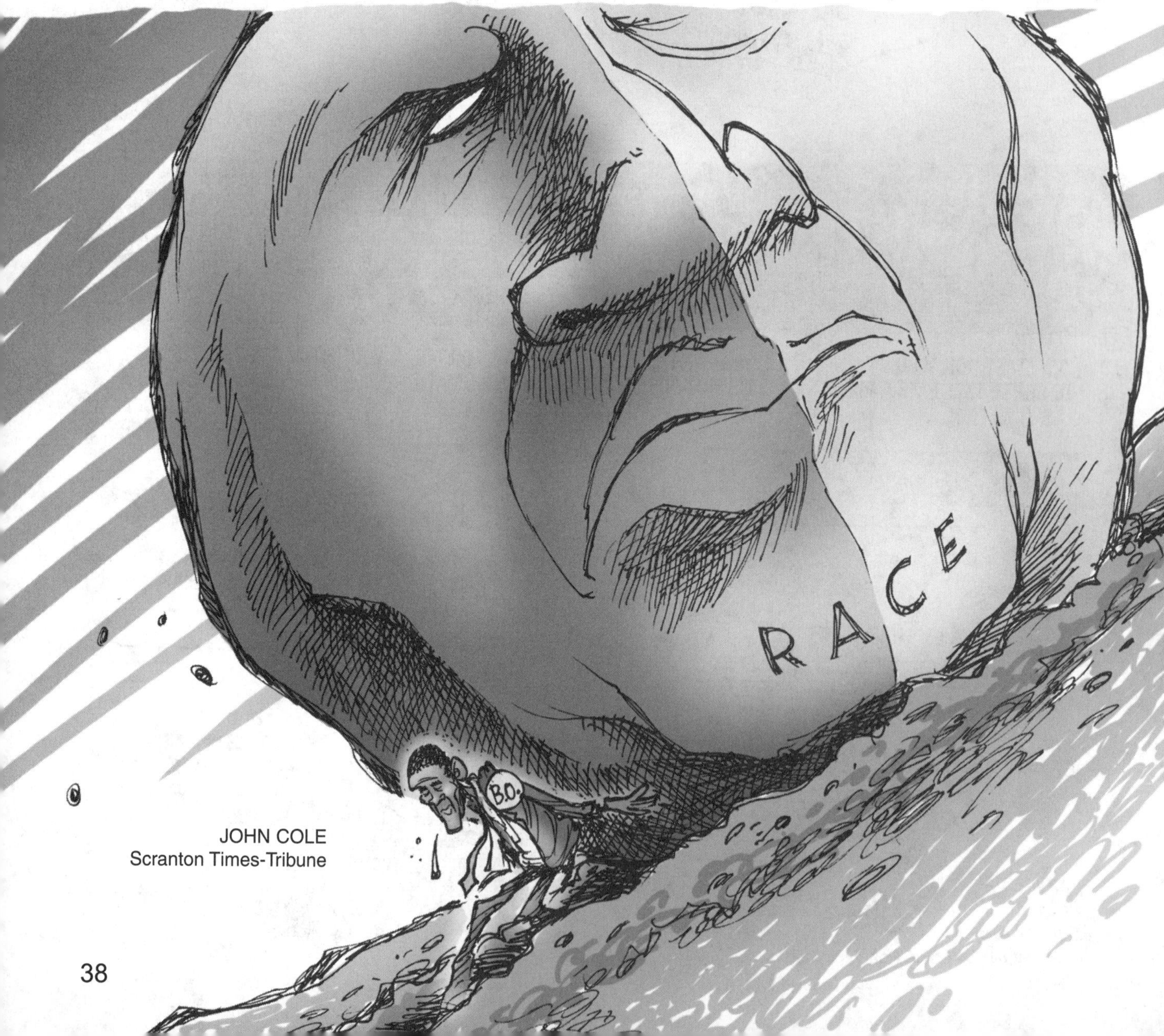

JOHN COLE
Scranton Times-Tribune

ARE YOU SAYING I'M NOT BLACK ENOUGH?
OH, SINCE I'M A WOMAN MY WEIGHT IS AN ISSUE?
RESPONDING to ACCUSATIONS OF BEING INEXPERIENCED LIGHTWEIGHTS
TREVER ALBUQUERQUE JOURNAL ©2008
Lemme see those blueprints again...
THE RACE CARD
THE GENDER CARD
HILLARY
OBAMA
UNDER CONSTRUCTION
2008 DEMOCRATIC PRESIDENTIAL CAMPAIGN HQ

ERIC ALLIE, Cagle Cartoons

JOHN TREVER
Albuquerque Journal

DARYL CAGLE
MSNBC.COM

I'M VOTING FOR OBAMA CUZ I'M BLACK AND HE'S BLACK.
I'M VOTING FOR HILLARY CUZ I'M A WOMAN AND SHE'S A WOMAN.
I'M VOTING FOR OBAMA CUZ I'M A BLACK WOMAN AND HE'S BLACK.
I'M VOTING FOR HILLARY CUZ I'M A LATINO WOMAN AND SHE'S NOT BLACK.
I'M VOTING FOR HUCKABEE CUZ JESUS TOLD ME TO.
I'M VOTING FOR ANYBODY BUT McCAIN CUZ I'M AN ANGRY CONSERVATIVE.
I'M VOTING FOR ROMNEY CUZ HE FLIP-FLOPS.
DARYL CAGLE MSNBC.com

RACE CARD

EricAllie
cnsnews.com
CagleCartoons.com
NORMAL
NORMAL
NORMAL
NORMAL
'08
IDENTITY POLITICS

ERIC ALLIE
Cagle Cartoons

GENDER CARD

NATE BEELER
Washington
Examiner

WHICH ROLE WILL YOU BE PLAYING TODAY MRS. CLINTON- WONDER WOMAN OR LITTLE BO PEEP?
© GARYMCCOY.ORG
2007 CAGLECARTOONS.COM

SCORECARD
CHANGE: 0
POLITICS AS USUAL: 1

GARY MCCOY, Cagle Cartoons

J.D. CROWE
Mobile Register

JOHN COLE, Scranton Times-Tribune

So Many Candidates

Every campaign season starts extra crowded, before the caucuses and primaries and respective fumbles take most of the candidates down. But this year the field was especially packed. Everyone was just so excited to follow George W. Bush's act! There wasn't much making sense of the field, though -- or, sometimes, even remembering who was who.

But after some tumultuous months, we were left with a Final 3 – Hillary Clinton, Barack Obama and John McCain – to duke it out until the bitter end.

R.J. MATSON
St. Louis Post Dispatch

PAT BAGLEY
Salt Lake Tribune (UT)

M.e. COHEN
Politicalcartoons.com

R.J. MATSON
St. Louis Post Dispatch

The GOP DISCOVERS ITS UNIFYING THEME...

...WE'RE TOAST..!

Z.

NATE BEELER
Washington
Examiner

R.J. MATSON
St. Louis
Post Dispatch

DARYL CAGLE
MSNBC.COM

J.D. CROWE
Mobile Register

DEMOLITION DERBY

HEY! MAKE ROOM FOR US!

MIKE KEEFE
Denver Post

www.caglecartoons.com

JIMMY MARGULIES, The Record (NJ)

TAYLOR JONES, El Nuevo Dia, Puerto Rico

Frontrunners...?

HEY!

MONTE WOLVERTON
Cagle Cartoons

caglecartoons.com

© 2008 MONTE WOLVERTON

PAVEL CONSTANTIN
Romania

THOMAS "TAB" BOLDT
Calgary Sun (Canada)

JOHN TREVER
Albuquerque Journal

SANDY HUFFAKER, Cagle Cartoons

JOE HELLER
Green Bay Press Gazette

JOHN TREVER, Albuquerque Journal

PATRICK CHAPPATTE
International Herald Tribune

RULES for CARTOONISTS...
1. DON'T DRAW OBAMA WITH BIG LIPS... THAT'S RACIST.

2. DON'T DRAW HILLARY WITH BIG HIPS... THAT'S SEXIST.

3. YOU CAN DRAW THE WHITE GUY, McCAIN'S FUNNY NECK ANY WAY YOU WANT.

DARYL CAGLE, MSNBC.COM

PARESH NATH, India

for the price of one

JIMMY MARGULIES, The Record (NJ)

PATRICK CORRIGAN
Toronto Star

GO CLINTON!...

THOMAS "TAB" BOLDT, Calgary Sun (Canada)

OLLE JOHANSSON, Sweden

FREDERICK DELIGNE
Nice-Matin, France

SANDY HUFFAKER, Cagle Cartoons

RIBER HANSSON
Sweden

A CLASSIC TALE, REVISITED...

H

FINISH

McCAIN

MLANE
www.caglecartoons.com

MIKE LANE, Cagle Cartoons

Super Tuesday

The first few primaries were a good litmus test, but Super Tuesday traditionally separates the presidential wheat from the chaff. For the GOP, it did just that. The Republicans whittled their field down to John McCain and a stubborn but statistically insignificant hanger-on, Mike Huckabee. But the Dems weren't so lucky. Hillary Clinton and Barack Obama racked up nearly identical numbers of delegates and emerged from the traditional campaign trail with meat grinder intact, and ready for more.

LARRY WRIGHT
Detroit News

JEFF PARKER, Florida Today

JOHN COLE, Scranton Times-Tribune

PAT BAGLEY, Salt Lake Tribune (UT)

R.J. MATSON, New York Observer

R.J. MATSON
St. Louis Post Dispatch

ADAM ZYGLIS
Buffalo News

GARY MCCOY, Cagle Cartoons

NATE BEELER, Washington Examiner

Super Tuesday Scouting Report
H.CLINTON, Tight End • Solid Performer • Ace Pass (Bill) catcher • Fakes Injury (cries) • Artful Blocker • All charges Dropped • Killer Instinct.

B.OBAMA, QB. Sees the whole field • Rocket Delivery • Few Rookie Mistakes • Great Offensive Line led by "MOOSE" Kennedy • No Sacks (Faithful).
Huffaker www.CAGLECARTOONS.COM

SANDY HUFFAKER, Cagle Cartoons

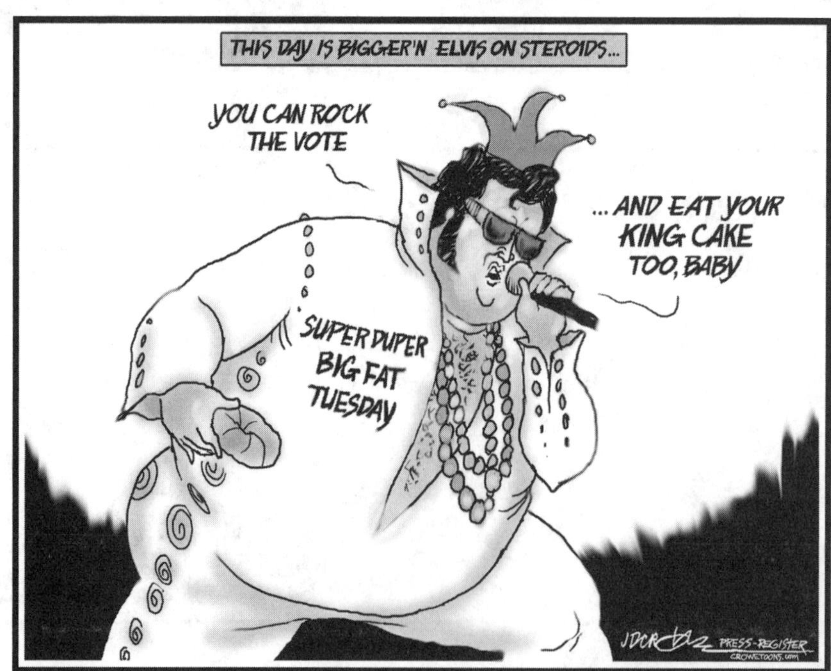
THIS DAY IS BIGGER'N ELVIS ON STEROIDS...
YOU CAN ROCK THE VOTE
...AND EAT YOUR KING CAKE TOO, BABY
SUPER DUPER BIG FAT TUESDAY
PRESS-REGISTER

J.D. CROWE
Mobile Register

JOHN TREVER
Albuquerque Journal

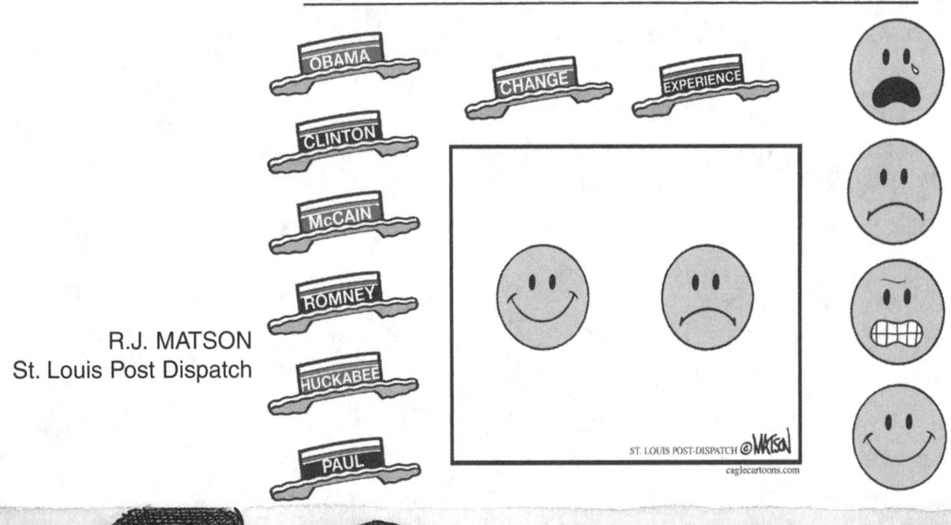

R.J. MATSON
St. Louis Post Dispatch

©Taylor Jones

TAYLOR JONES
Politicalcartoons.com

Mitt Romney

Former Massachusetts Gov. Mitt Romney came raring out of the starting gate, but lost steam further down the campaign trail. He had a strong showing in the early caucuses and primaries in Iowa, Wyoming, and New Hampshire. But Romney's Mormonism was a serious turnoff even for the fiercely Christian GOP voter base – but what a turn-on for cartoonists!

By the time Super Tuesday had rolled around, Mitt was out for the count; and just one week later he threw his support to front-runner John McCain.

THE AMAZING MITT
BEHOLD HIS STANDS ON:
•ABORTION
•GAY MARRIAGE
•GUN CONTROL
•IMMIGRATION
Taylor Jones 2007
©Taylor Jones

TAYLOR JONES
Politicalcartoons.com

PAT BAGLEY, Salt Lake Tribune (UT)

PAT BAGLEY
Salt Lake Tribune (UT)

ADAM ZYGLIS
Buffalo News

PAT BAGLEY
Salt Lake Tribune (UT)

BRIAN FAIRRINGTON
Cagle Cartoons

BOB ENGLEHART
Hartford Courant

PAT BAGLEY
Salt Lake Tribune (UT)

PAT BAGLEY
Salt Lake Tribune (UT)

BRIAN FAIRRINGTON
Cagle Cartoons

J.D. CROWE
Mobile Register

PAT BAGLEY
Salt Lake Tribune (UT)

PAT BAGLEY
Salt Lake Tribune (UT)

WITH A MORMON IN THE RACE, REPUBLICANS BUSY THEMSELVES WITH THE QUESTION — WHO WOULD JESUS ENDORSE?

PAT BAGLEY
Salt Lake Tribune
(UT)

BRIAN FAIRRINGTON
Cagle Cartoons

BRIAN FAIRRINGTON
Cagle Cartoons

SANDY HUFFAKER, Cagle Cartoons

ADAM ZYGLIS
Buffalo News

DARYL CAGLE
MSNBC.COM

NATE BEELER
Washington Examiner

RETURNS

SORRY, FOLKS.... WE DON'T ACCEPT DAMAGED GOODS.

Mitt

Hillary

BEELER ©07 The Washington Examiner CAGLECARTOONS.com

JIMMY MARGULIES, The Record (NJ)

DARYL CAGLE
MSNBC.COM

R.J. MATSON
St. Louis Post Dispatch

Presidential Primaries

Hillary and Obama battled state by state. Michigan and Florida loomed as a problem for the Democrats who refused to count their votes (for Hillary). While most eyes were on the tumultuous Democratic Party, for their part the Republicans had a pretty exciting primary race of their own. John McCain, Mitt Romney, Rudy Giuliani, and Mike Huckabee battled it out for the Republican nomination with no holds barred. Each one got a turn at the front of the pack, -- until one misstep or another took them down, one by one.

WIS-minster Dog Show ~ *Your guide to the Wisconsin Primary*

RETRIEVER

DELEGATES

PINSCHER

CAMPAIGN FUNDS

GREYHOUND

McC

POINTER

HE'S NO CONSERV-ATIVE

HUCK

JOE HELLER
Green Bay Press Gazette

Mike Keefe THE DENVER POST 5·31·08

AND SO, BY REARRANGING THE TERMS, WE CAN REACH ANY DESIRED TOTAL IN THE SUM OF THIS INFINITE SERIES!

TRUE. BUT THIS IS FINITE MATH CLASS, HILLARY.

=NOMINA

PRIMARIES

CAUCUSES

POPVOTE

MIRACLE

HOCUS POCUS

fudge

ROUNDING ERROR

RULES

MIKE KEEFE
Denver Post

www.caglecartoons.com

WHY I WENT TO BED EARLY

THIS IS INTERESTING... A MAJORITY OF VOTERS IN OHIO WANT CLINTON TO ANSWER THE RED PHONE AT 3:00A.M.
OHIO CLINTON ✔ OBAMA ☐

BUT IF THE PHONE IS RINGING IN THE WHITE HOUSE AT 2:00A.M. VOTERS IN TEXAS FEEL SAFER WITH OBAMA.
TEXAS CLINTON ☐ OBAMA ✔

AND IF THE PHONE RINGS ANYTIME AFTER 6:00AM. AND BEFORE NOON RHODE ISLAND PICKS McCAIN.
RHODE ISLAND McCAIN ✔

WHICH BEGS THE QUESTION: WHO DO VERMONTERS WANT TAKING THAT CALL AT 2:30 ON A PERFECT SKI DAY?
VERMONT UNDECIDED
©MATSON
caglecartoons.com ROLL CALL

R.J. MATSON, Roll Call

caglecartoons.com
1
2

LARRY WRIGHT
Detroit News

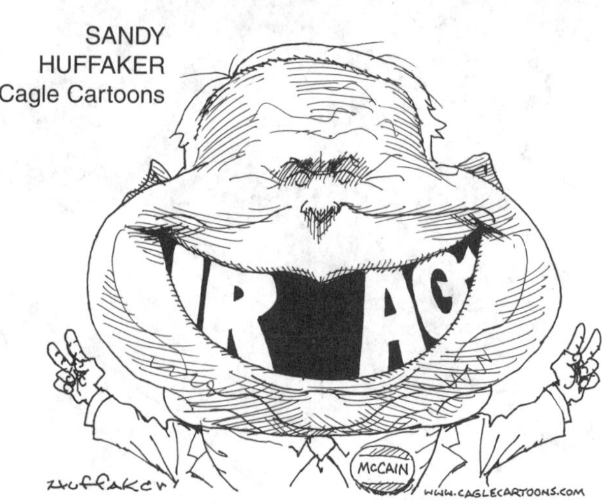
huffaker
McCAIN
www.caglecartoons.com

SANDY
HUFFAKER
Cagle Cartoons

JOHN COLE
Scranton
Times-Tribune

R.J. MATSON, St. Louis Post Dispatch

"WHAT ARE WE WAITING FOR, EXACTLY?"

PAT BAGLEY, Salt Lake Tribune (UT)

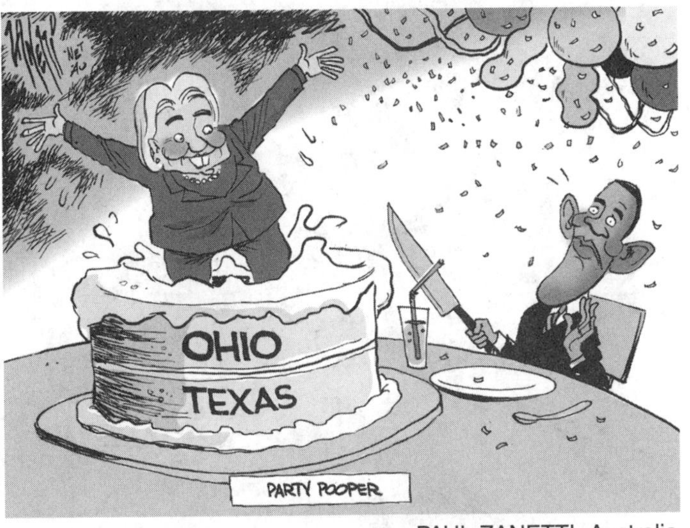

PAUL ZANETTI, Australia

JOHN COLE
Scranton
Times-Tribune

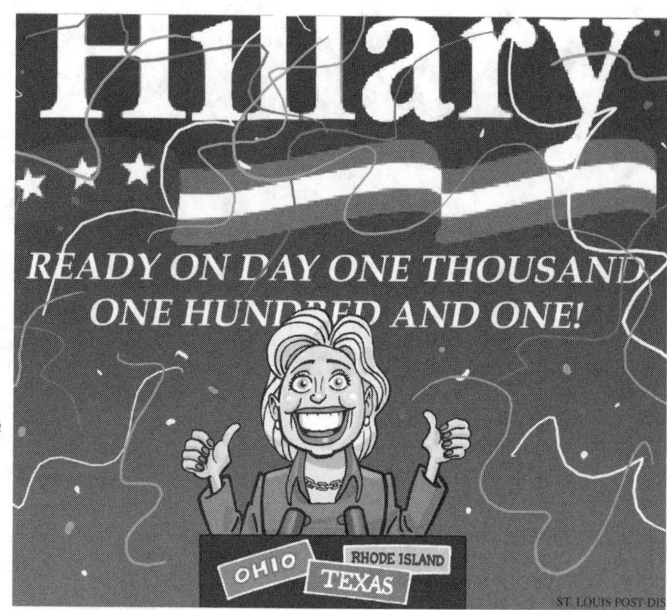

"MY CAMPAIGN IS JUST GETTING STARTED!"

R.J. MATSON, St. Louis Post Dispatch

OLLE JOHANSSON
Sweden

J.D. CROWE, Mobile Register

TAYLOR JONES, El Nuevo Dia, Puerto Rico

ADAM ZYGLIS, Buffalo News

JIMMY MARGULIES, The Record (NJ)

JOHN COLE, Scranton Times-Tribune

JOHN DARKOW
Columbia Daily Tribune (MO)

LARRY WRIGHT, Detroit News

JOHN TREVER, Albuquerque Journal

R.J. MATSON, Roll Call

"I GOT IT! I GOT IT! I GOT IT!..."

PETAR PISMESTROVIC
Austria

LARRY WRIGHT, Detroit News

JOHN TREVER, Albuquerque Journal

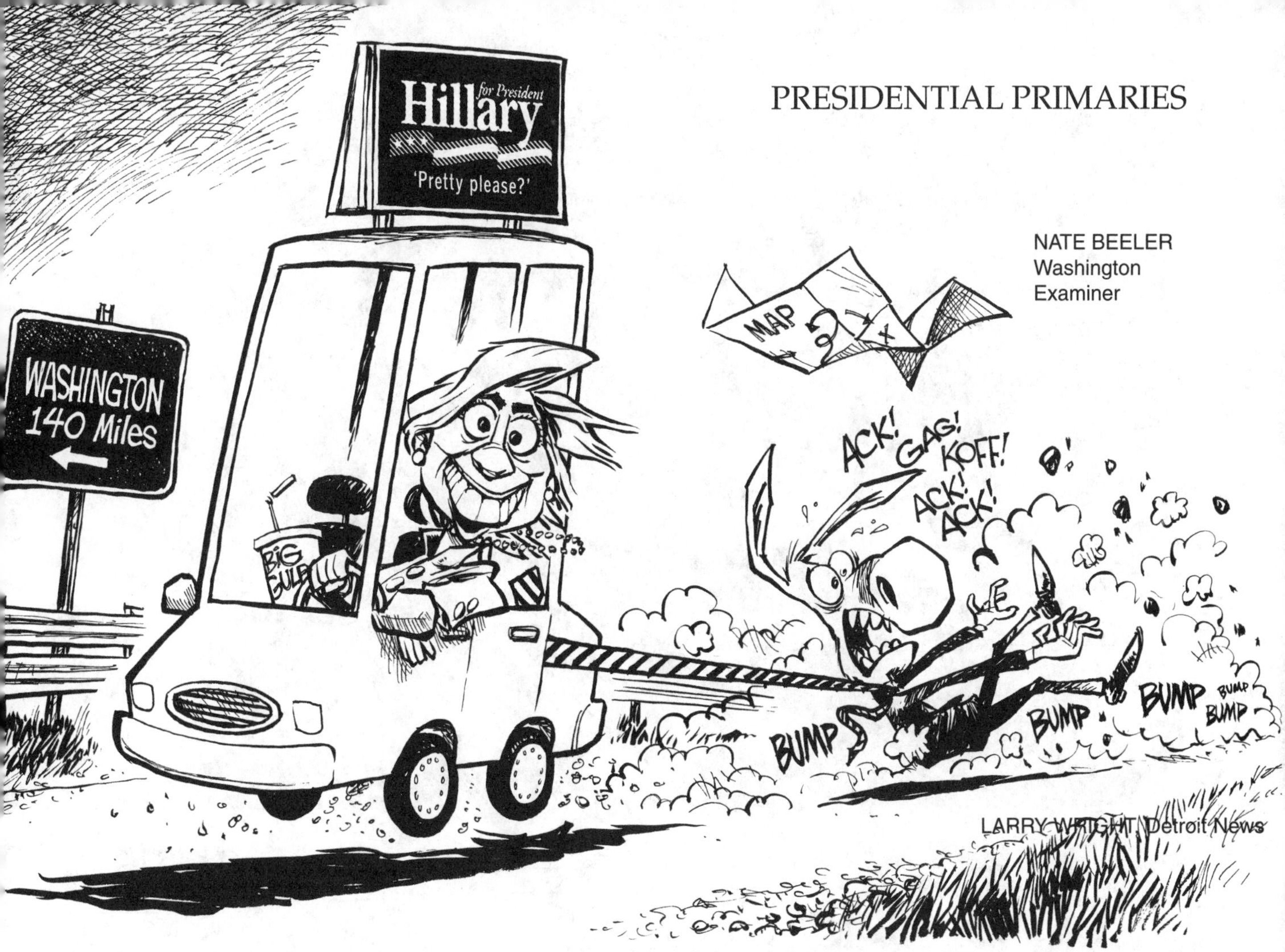

Hillary for President
'Pretty please?'

NATE BEELER
Washington
Examiner

MAP

WASHINGTON
140 Miles

BIG GULP

ACK! GAG! KOFF! ACK! ACK!

BUMP BUMP BUMP BUMP BUMP

LARRY WRIGHT, Detroit News

"IT'S A LOOOOOOONG ROAD TO 1600 PENNSYLVANIA AVENUE!"

WE CAN'T JUST UP AND COUNT PRIMARY VOTES IN MICHIGAN AND FLORIDA!
IF WE DID WE'D HAVE TO ADD TWO MORE STARS TO ALL OF OUR TRADITIONAL 48-STAR FLAGS!

LARRY WRIGHT
Detroit News

BUS DUEL
PENNSYLVANIA PRIMARY
CLINTON
OBAMA
©MATSON
NEW YORK OBSERVER
caglecartoons.com

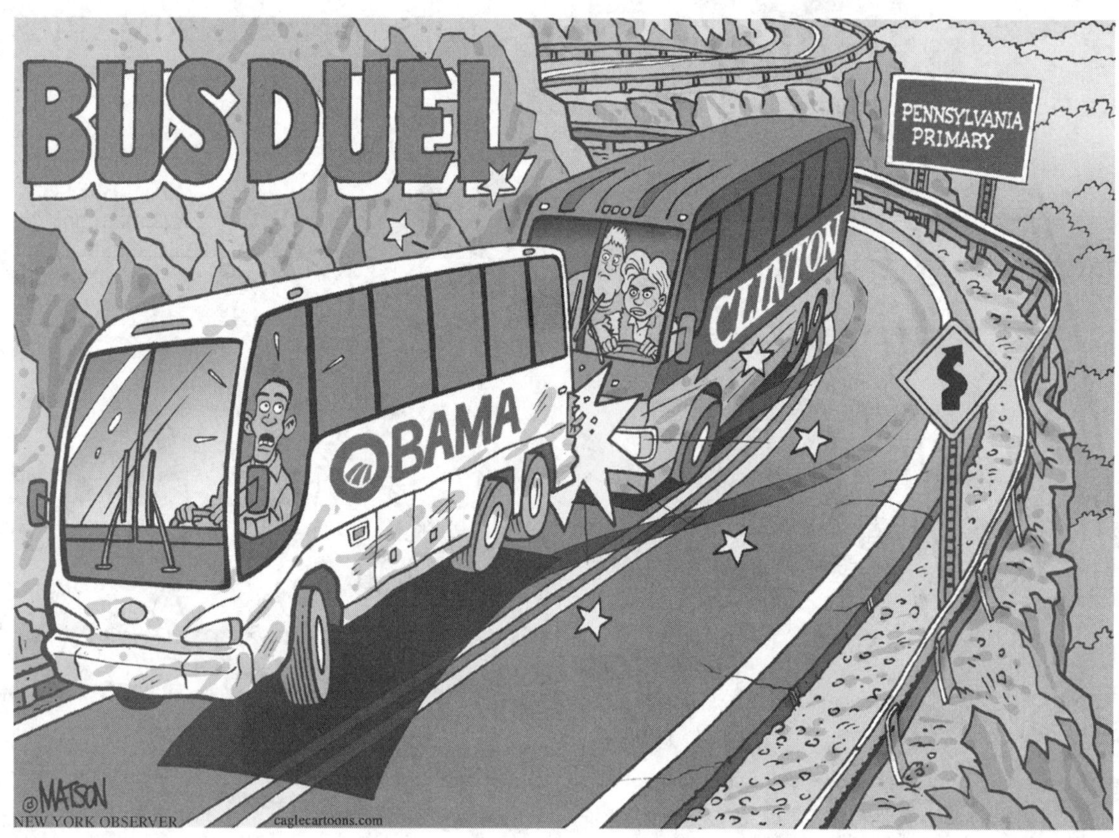

R.J. MATSON
New York
Observer

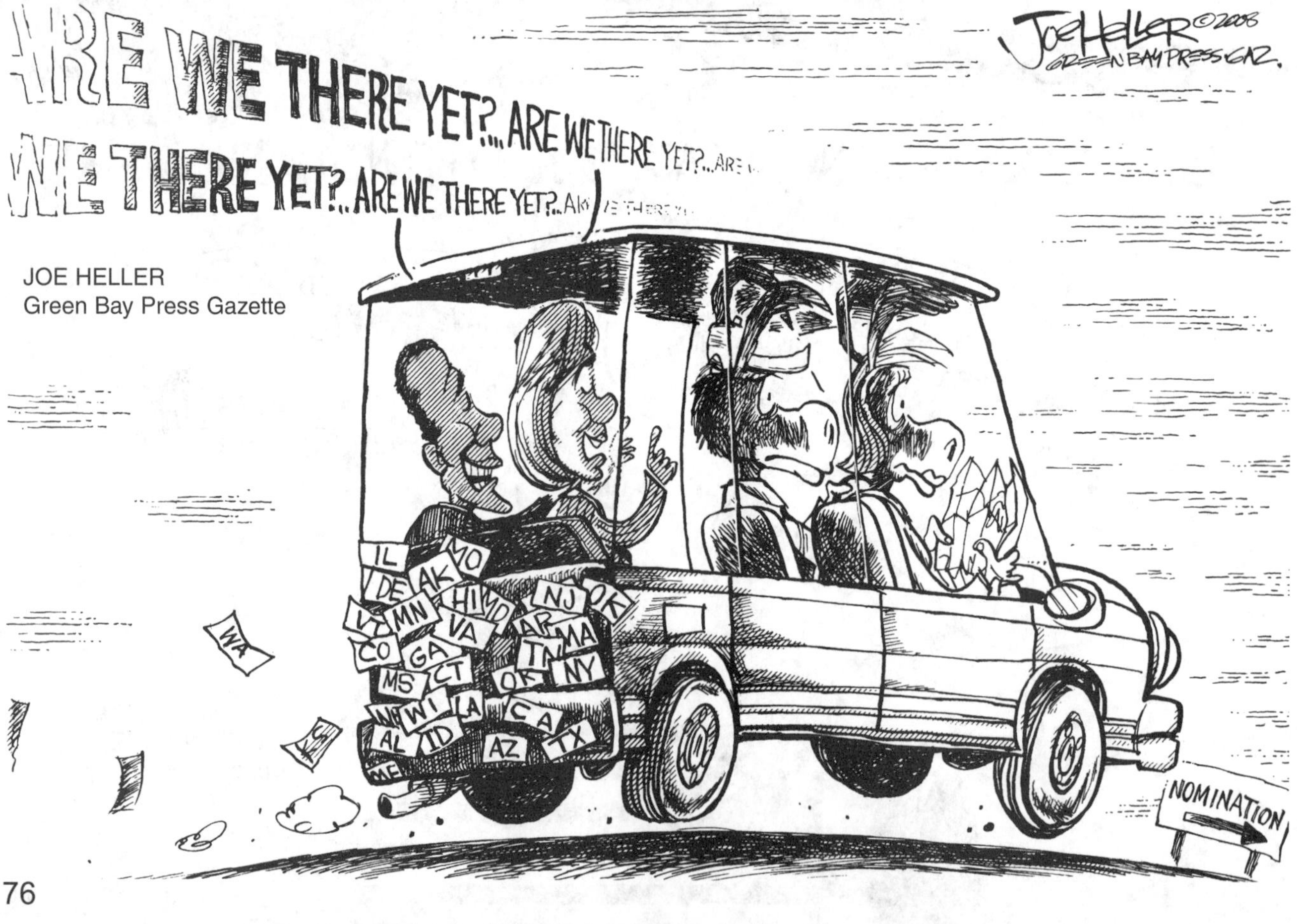

JOE HELLER ©2008
GREEN BAY PRESS GAZ.
ARE WE THERE YET?... ARE WE THERE YET?...
WE THERE YET?.. ARE WE THERE YET?..
IL
MO
DE
AK
MN
HI
MD
NJ
OK
VT
VA
AR
MA
WA
CO
GA
TN
NY
MS
CT
OH
WI
LA
CA
AL
ID
AZ
TX
KS
NOMINATION

JOE HELLER
Green Bay Press Gazette

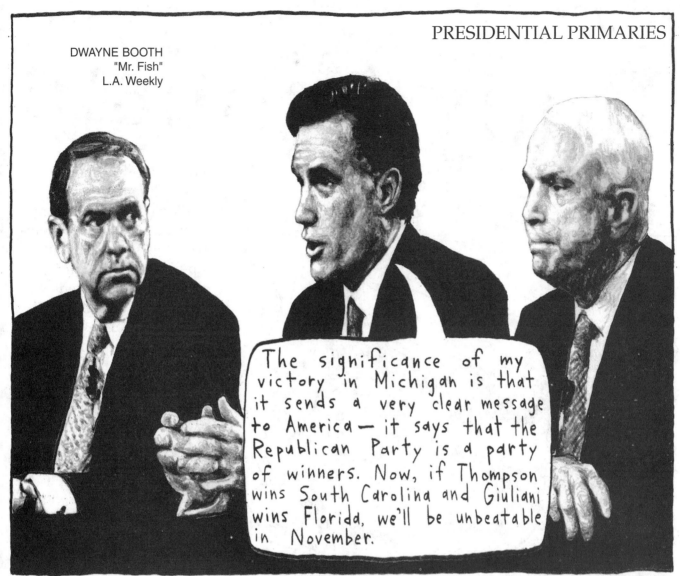

DWAYNE BOOTH
"Mr. Fish"
L.A. Weekly

The significance of my victory in Michigan is that it sends a very clear message to America—it says that the Republican Party is a party of winners. Now, if Thompson wins South Carolina and Giuliani wins Florida, we'll be unbeatable in November.

MR.FISH

ADAM ZYGLIS
Buffalo News

R.J. MATSON, New York Observer

STILL STANDING

Rudy Giuliani

TAYLOR JONES
Politicalcartoons.com
Taylor Jones 2007
DIVORCE DECREE
DIVORCE DECREE

There for a while, Rudolph Giuliani, the former New York City mayor who couldn't go a day without invoking the terrible memory of 9/11, was shaping up to be the Republican nominee for president. After announcing his candidacy, Rudy sailed through 2007 at the front of the polls, and he even picked up an unlikely endorsement from televangelist Pat Robertson.

But then Giuliani stumbled in a series of well-publicized missteps, including the tens of thousands in city bills the former mayor racked up while visiting his then-mistress (later, wife), Judith Nathan. Giuliani really shot himself in the foot by focusing on later, bigger primaries instead of the earlier, more influential ones. It was a disappointing moment for cartoonists who had high hopes for a cross-dresser in the White House.

IN AN AWKWARDLY STAGED MOMENT RUDY RECEIVES A CELL PHONE CALL FROM HIS WIFE.

IN AN AWKWARDLY NOT STAGED MOMENT RUDY RECEIVES CELL PHONE CALLS FROM HIS FIRST, SECOND, AND THIRD WIFE AT THE SAME TIME.

M.e. COHEN Politicalcartoons.com

JIMMY MARGULIES, The Record (NJ)

CHRISTO KOMARNITSKI, Bulgaria

R.J. MATSON, St. Louis Post Dispatch

M.e. COHEN
Politicalcartoons.com

JOHN DARKOW
Columbia Daily Tribune (MO)

JIMMY MARGULIES
The Record (NJ)

R.J. MATSON
New York Observer

"GOD KNOWS, I'M NOT THE *ONLY* REPUBLICAN WITH PROBLEMS..."

BOB ENGLEHART
Hartford Courant

HAPPINESS IS A WARM CANDIDATE

JEFF
PARKER
Florida Today

JOHN DARKOW
Columbia Daily
Tribune (MO)

JIMMY MARGULIES
The Record (NJ)

J.D. CROWE
Mobile Register

3:00 a.m. Phone Calls

Hillary Clinton's camp truly fumbled with their television scare-ad featuring cute, sleeping kids completely unaware of a desperate middle-of-the-night phone call made to their president, Hillary. The ad didn't exactly say that Barack Obama would sleep through the call and let the terrorists win, but it didn't need to. The 3:00 a.m. phone call ad became the bad-campaigning cautionary tale of the season and signaled the downward slide of Hillary's increasingly desperate campaign.

R.J. MATSON, Roll Call

"IF YOUR MOMMY AND DADDY VOTE FOR OBAMA, THE REPUBLICANS WILL EAT YOU ALIVE AND THE TERRORISTS WILL BLOW US ALL UP!!"

JOHN DARKOW, Columbia Daily Tribune (MO)

SANDY HUFFAKER, Cagle Cartoons

Who do you want listening in on your call?

JIMMY MARGULIES The Record (NJ)

MONTE WOLVERTON, Cagle Cartoons

Superdelegates

It was the word on all the pundits' lips this campaign season, but before 2008, many Americans had never even heard of these tie-breaking superdelegates. Most primary races had never been close enough to require their use, yet suddenly they were deciding the future of the Democratic Party, and potentially the country. What was this weird system, and who were these powerful voters and just how could Barack and Hillary court them without the appearance of impropriety?

BRIAN FAIRRINGTON
Cagle Cartoons

JIMMY MARGULIES
The Record (NJ)

SANDY HUFFAKER
Cagle Cartoons

MIKE KEEFE, Denver Post

JOHN TREVER, Albuquerque Journal

MIKE KEEFE
Denver Post

SANDY HUFFAKER
Cagle Cartoons

JOHN COLE
Scranton
Times-Tribune

MIKE KEEFE
Denver Post

JOE HELLER
Green Bay Press Gazette

IAIN GREEN

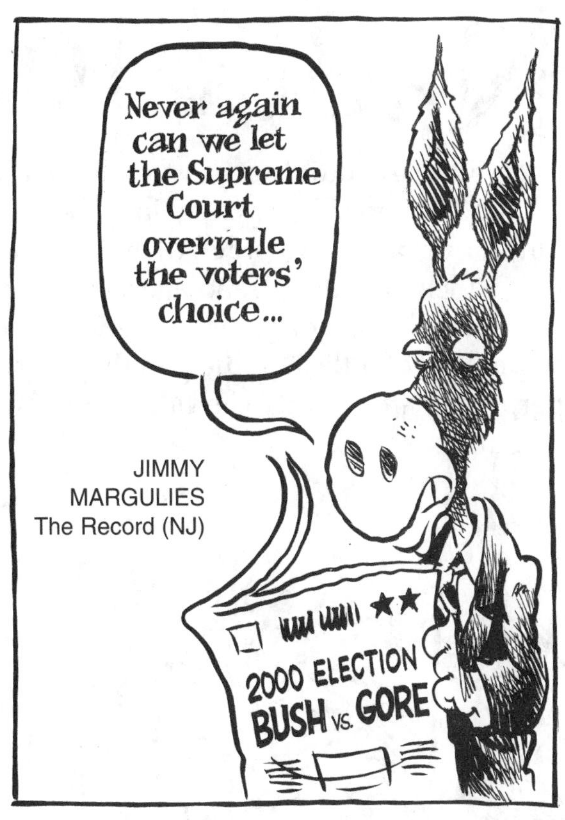

JIMMY MARGULIES
The Record (NJ)

J.D. CROWE, Mobile Register

M.e. COHEN, Politicalcartoons.com

Nader for President

There was an audible groan from both blue coasts when Ralph Nader announced he'd be running for president yet again. After a divisive race in 2000 (one which many still blame him for tipping to George W.) and the lackluster follow-up in 2004, most Democrats thought (hoped?) he wouldn't sabotage their attempt to take back the White House. But the Dems were actually so crazy eyed and desperate with their internal fighting that Nader became something of a flash in the pan this year—Barack and Hillary were too exciting for the perpetual Green Party candidate to get much time in the limelight.

NADER
Huffaker www.caglecartoons.com
I HAVE DECIDED AGAIN TO RUN FOR PRESIDENT...
WHERE'S THE ACADEMY AWARDS ORCHESTRA WHEN YOU NEED IT...?!
NEWS LIVE
NADER

SANDY HUFFAKER
Cagle Cartoons

NATE BEELER
Washington Examiner

The Nader Political Animal
GOP BACKING
DEM VOTES
RALPH

MIKE LANE
Cagle Cartoons

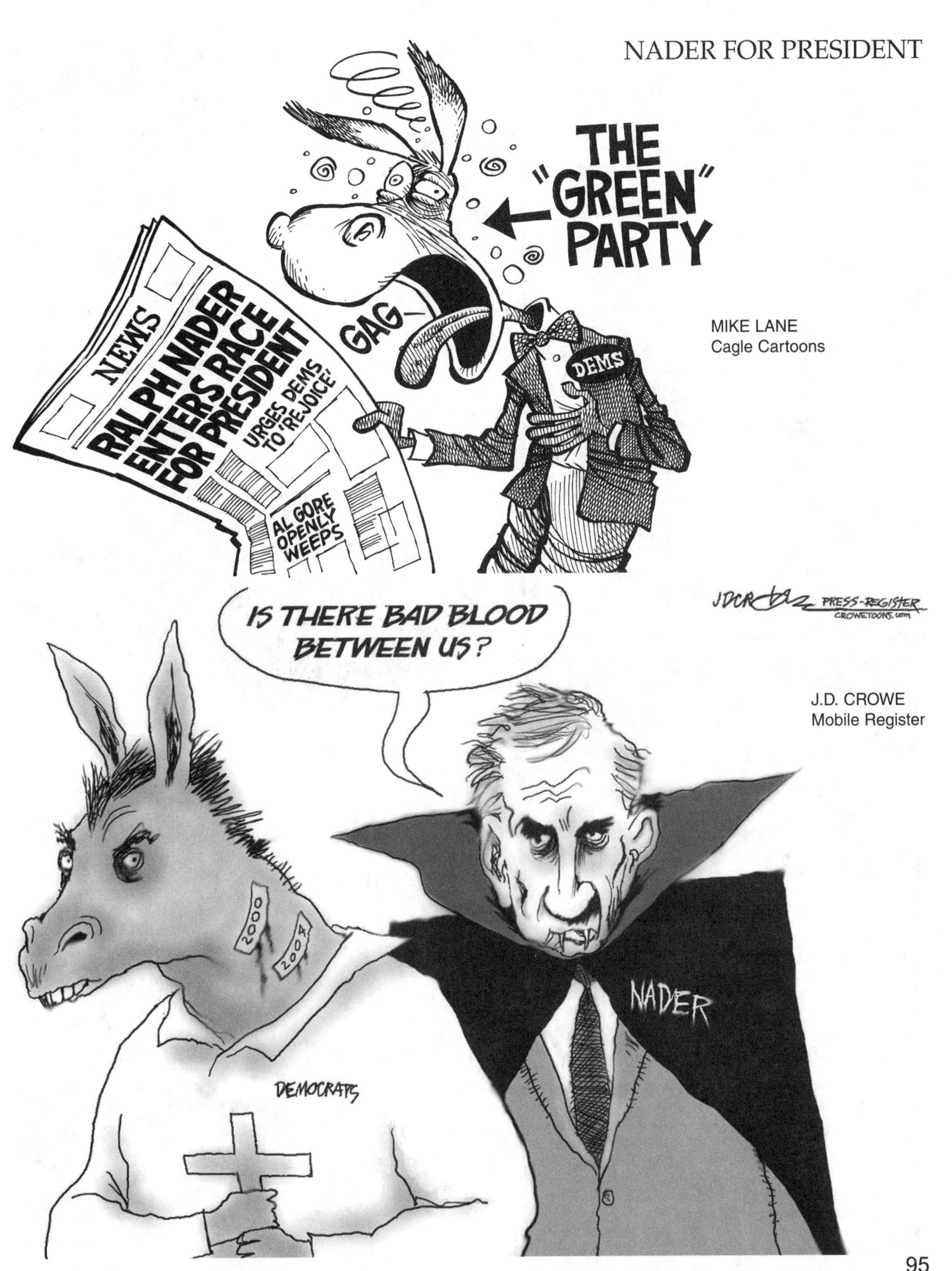

MIKE LANE
Cagle Cartoons

J.D. CROWE
Mobile Register

IF THEY SAY "DON'T RUN," THEY'RE REALLY SAYING "DON'T SPEAK!"
NADER
caglecartoons.com

THAT'S EVEN BETTER
NADER
©2/1/08 HARTFORD COURANT.

BOB ENGLEHART
Hartford Courant
courant.com/boblog

na·dir (nā'dər) *n.*
1 *the lowest point of anything...*
ME FOR PRESIDENT

PAT BAGLEY
Salt Lake Tribune (UT)

VOTE NADER
UNSAFE AT ANY AGE

LARRY WRIGHT
Detroit News

AMATEURS...
SUPER DELEGATES
COULD THEY FOIL THE ELECTION?
2008 NADER
2004
2000

ADAM ZYGLIS, Buffalo News

BOB ENGLEHART
Hartford Courant

MIKE LANE
Cagle Cartoons

MIKE LANE, Cagle Cartoons

JIMMY MARGULIES, The Record (NJ)

R.J. MATSON, St. Louis Post Dispatch

SANDY HUFFAKER
Cagle Cartoons

JOHN TREVER
Albuquerque Journal

John Edwards

After running as John Kerry's vice-presidential ticket mate in 2004, many expected John Edwards to make a stronger showing in the '08 race. Although everyone had been kind of disturbed by Kerry's woodenness, Edwards always seemed like a nice, side-parted young man, and he genuinely energized a lot of poor, white Americans. He held in strong toward the start, but faltered as the field grew more crowded with louder voices. Between his "Two Americas" cliché and one very expensive haircut, Edwards was soon made quick cartoon fodder – and even sooner pushed to the sidelines by Hillary and Barack. But Edwards ended up making bigger headlines after he dropped out of the race, when the press learned of his affair with a former staffer. Edwards bumbled through apologies while cartoonists were torn -- water under the bridge, or the end of a political career? Either way, it's always fun to watch the pretty ones fall.

HUFFAKER WWW.CAGLECARTOONS.COM

The Cost of a Haircut These Days...

Giuliani: WD-40, $5.50

Edwards: $400

Fred Thompson: NO CHARGE

Biden: $3,575

Hillary: $350.

W: Nappy cut, $250.

Britney: (DOES HER OWN)

Obama: $5.75

Romney $750.

K. Sheikh Mohammed: TOTAL WAX, $4,375.50

SANDY HUFFAKER
Cagle Cartoons

$400 HAIRCUT →
← $315,000 SMILE
COURTESY OF ALABAMA TRIAL LAWYERS
EDWARDS
PICK YOUR OUTRAGE.
JOHN EDWARD'S $400 DOLLAR BAD HAIRCUT.
GEORGE BUSH'S $400 BILLION DOLLAR BAD WAR.
M.e. COHEN

J.D. CROWE
Mobile Register

M.e. COHEN
Politicalcartoons.com

LARRY WRIGHT, Detroit News

DAVID FITZSIMMONS
Arizona Daily Star

J.D. CROWE
Mobile Register

JOHN COLE
Scranton
Times-Tribune

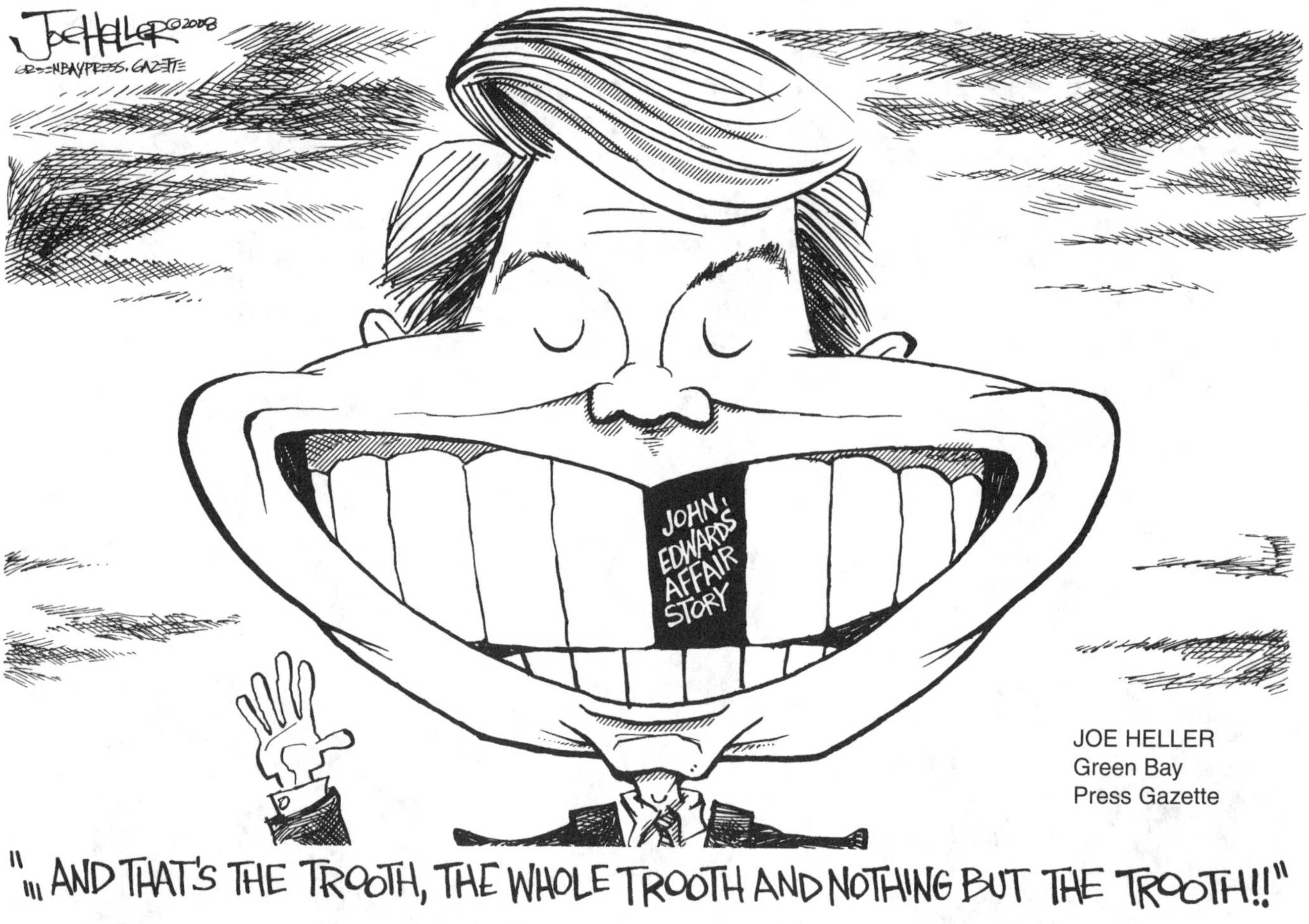

JoeHeller ©2008
GREENBAYPRESS.GAZETTE
JOHN EDWARDS' AFFAIR STORY
"... AND THAT'S THE TROOTH, THE WHOLE TROOTH AND NOTHING BUT THE TROOTH!!"

JOE HELLER
Green Bay
Press Gazette

SEX SCANDAL
EDWARDS
TWO AMERICAS
ERIC ALLIE

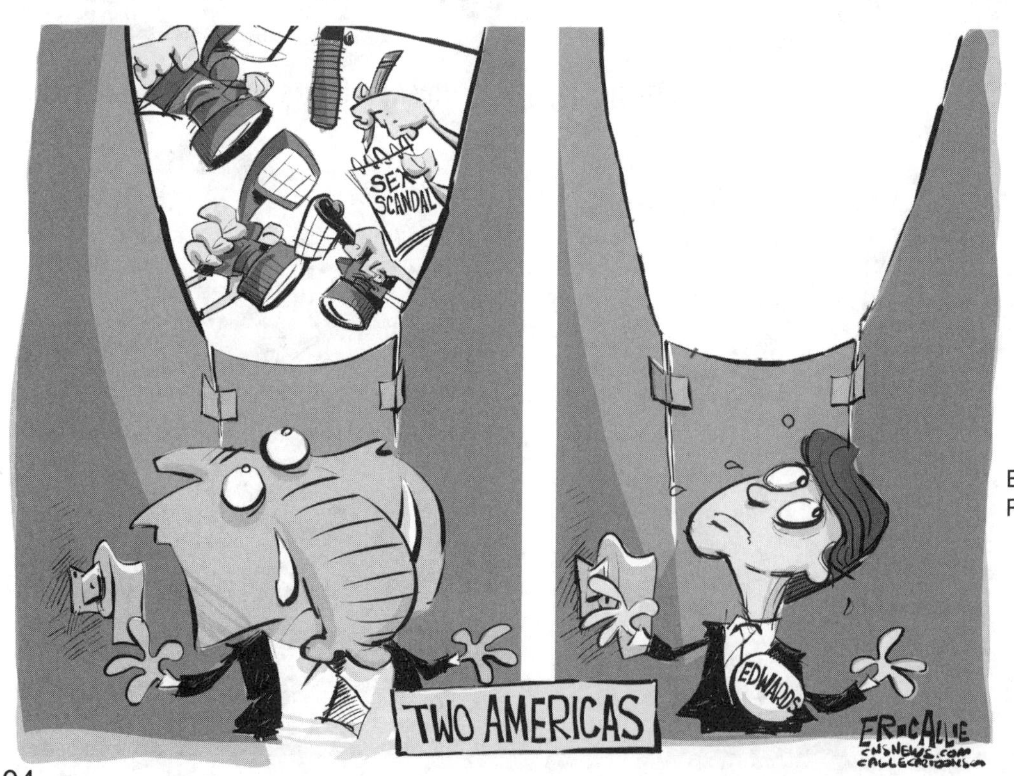

ERIC ALLIE
Politicalcartoons.com

GARY MCCOY
Cagle Cartoons

GARY MCCOY
Cagle Cartoons

JOHN EDWARDS' TWO AMERICAS

RANDY BISH
Pittsburgh Tribune-Review

ERIC ALLIE
Politicalcartoons.com

John Edwards Reveals
what he meant by the "Two Americas"
The Faithful
The Not so Faithful
8/11
DARKOW
COLUMBIA DAILY TRIBUNE
CAGLECARTOONS.COM

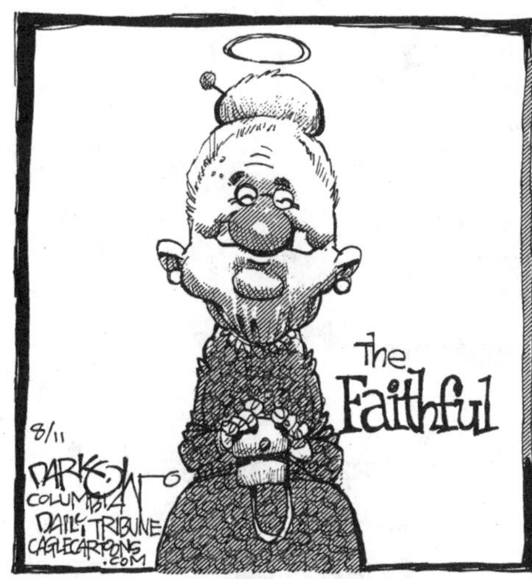

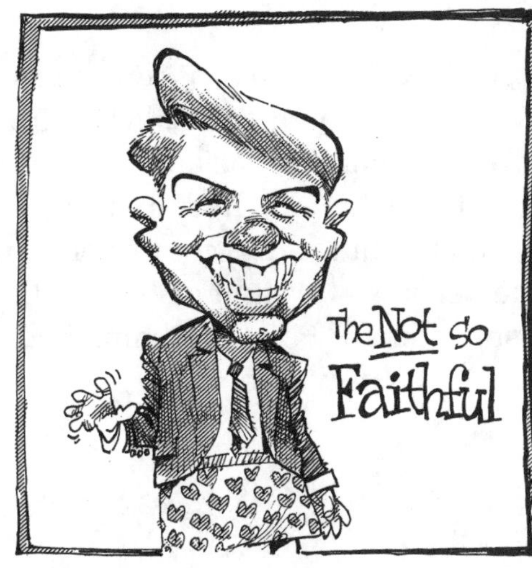

JOHN DARKOW
Columbia Daily Tribune
(MO)

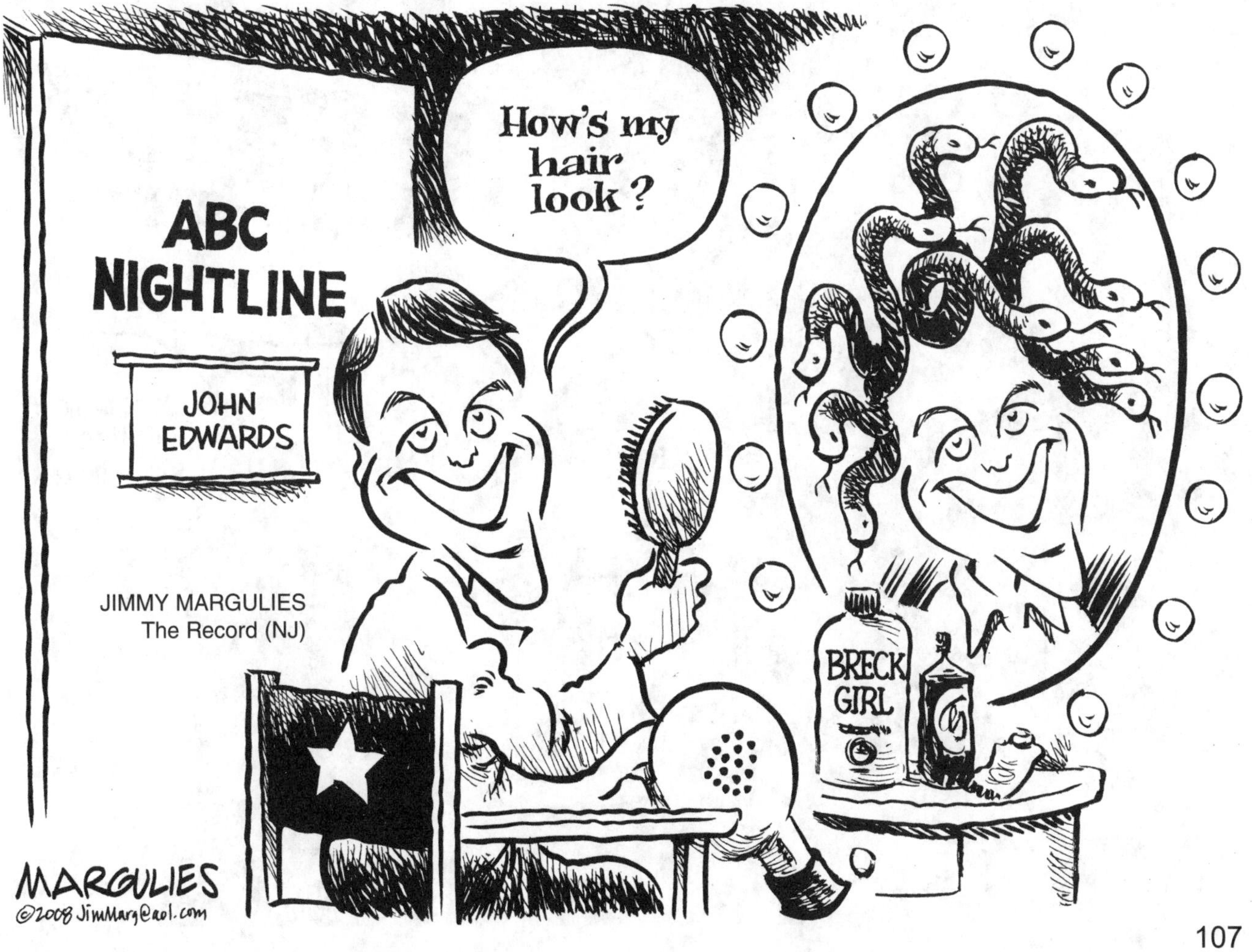

How's my hair look?
ABC NIGHTLINE
JOHN EDWARDS
BRECK GIRL
MARGULIES
©2008 JimMarg@aol.com

JIMMY MARGULIES
The Record (NJ)

Obama's Preacher

Barack Obama's former pastor, Rev. Jeremiah Wright, was a thorn in the presidential hopeful's side for some months. When the media found sound bites of Rev. Wright making racially charged comments, they plastered them all over the networks. In response, Obama was initially supportive of the Reverend; but as the controversy dragged on, and it became unclear whether it was Wright or the media who was dragging it, their relationship soured. Finally, Obama had to denounce his former pastor, lest he be taken down, too.

BRIAN FAIRRINGTON, Cagle Cartoons

TAYLOR JONES, Politicalcartoons.com

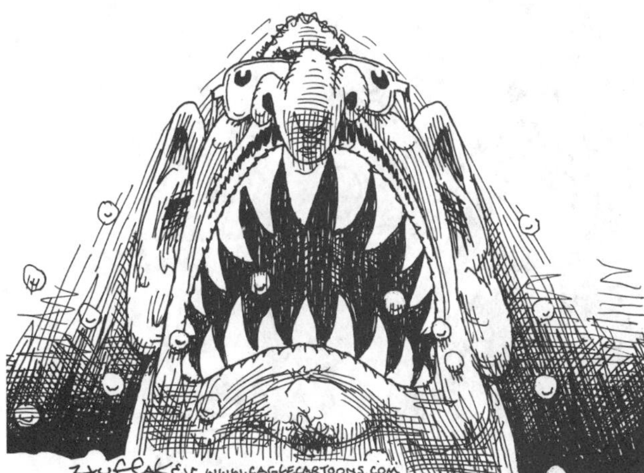

SANDY HUFFAKER, Cagle Cartoons

MIKE KEEFE
Denver Post

JOHN DARKOW, Columbia Daily Tribune (MO)

DARYL CAGLE, MSNBC.COM

ERIC ALLIE
Politicalcartoons.com

JOHN TREVER
Albuquerque Journal

JIMMY MARGULIES
The Record (NJ)

DARYL CAGLE
MSNBC.COM

BOB ENGLEHART
Hartford Courant

GARY MCCOY, Cagle Cartoons

JOHN COLE
Scranton Times-Tribune

SANDY HUFFAKER, Cagle Cartoons

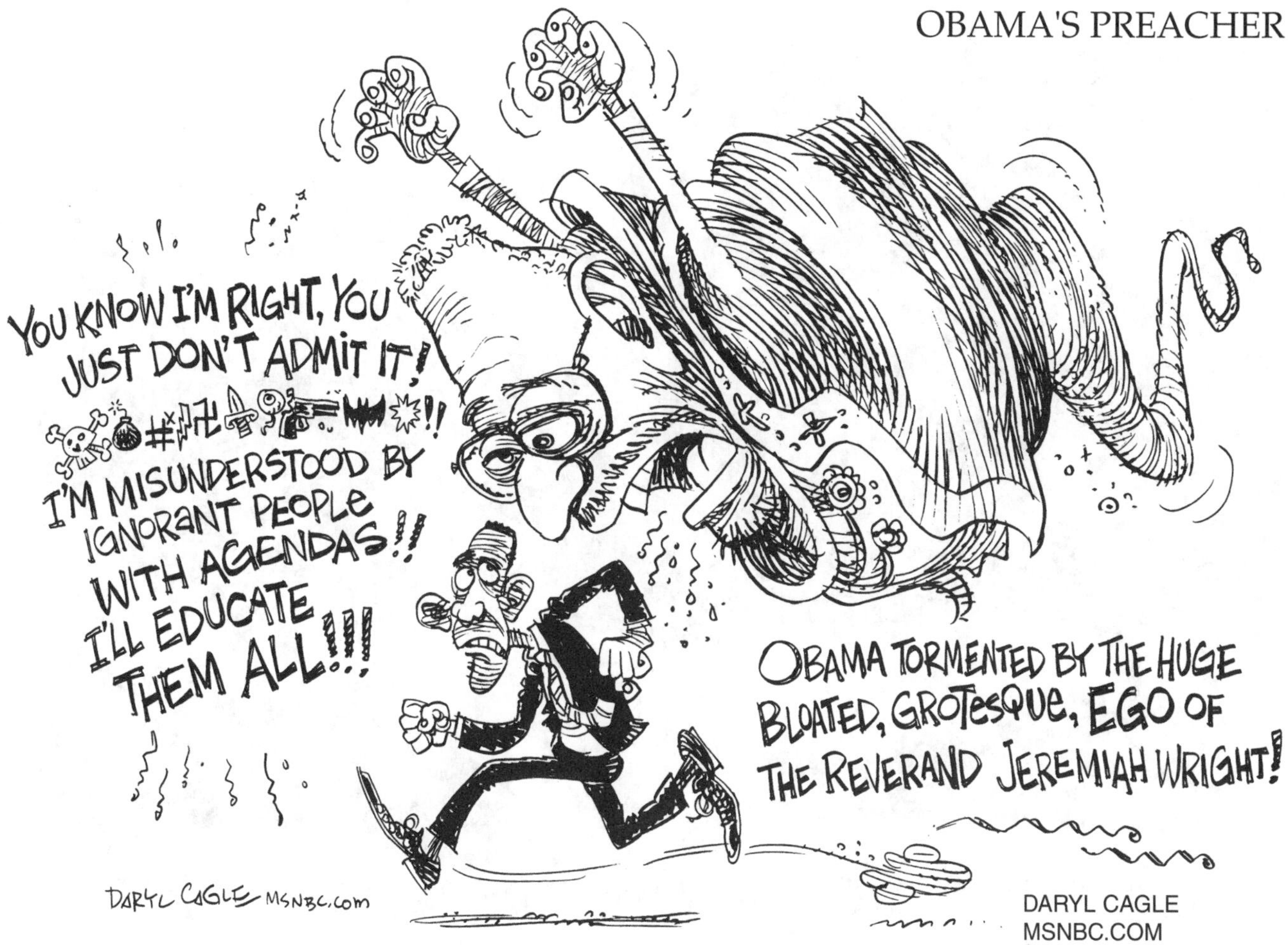

YOU KNOW I'M RIGHT, YOU JUST DON'T ADMIT IT!
I'M MISUNDERSTOOD BY IGNORANT PEOPLE WITH AGENDAS!! I'LL EDUCATE THEM ALL!!!
OBAMA TORMENTED BY THE HUGE BLOATED, GROTESQUE, EGO OF THE REVEREND JEREMIAH WRIGHT!
DARYL CAGLE MSNBC.com

DARYL CAGLE
MSNBC.COM

LET'S SEE NOW..
WHERE WAS I?... BEFORE I WAS SO RUDELY INTERRUPTED...
Obama

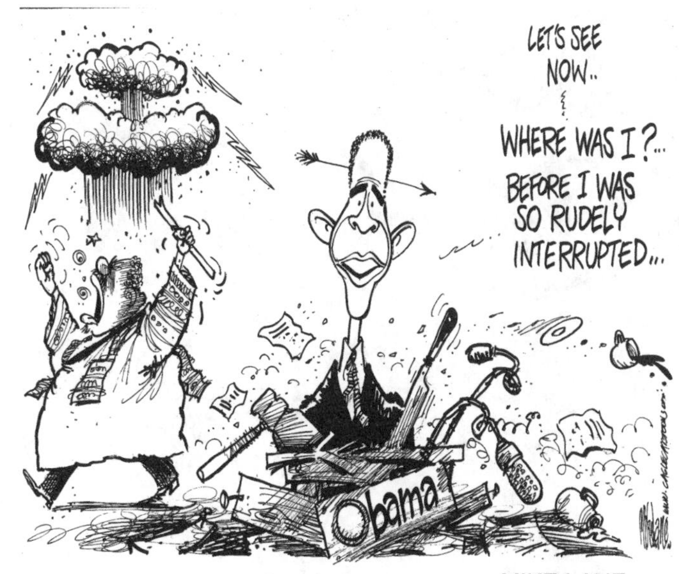

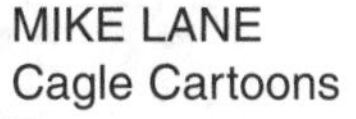

MIKE LANE
Cagle Cartoons

WRIGHT
caglecartoons.com courant.com/boblog

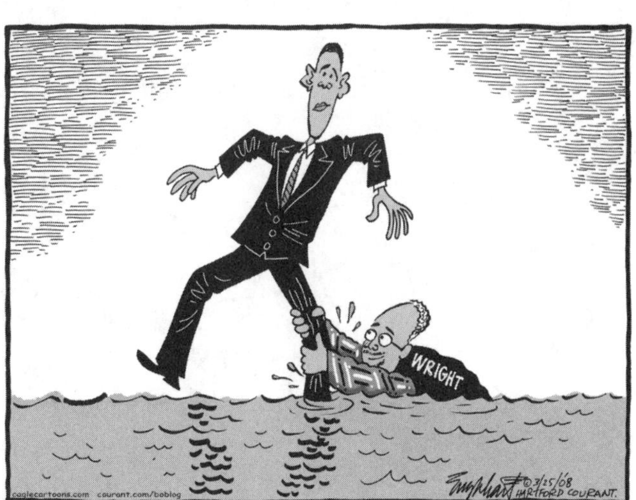

BOB ENGLEHART
Hartford Courant

"THANKS FOR WARMING UP MY AUDIENCE, KID. I'LL TAKE IT FROM HERE."

PAT BAGLEY
Salt Lake Tribune

GARY MCCOY
Cagle Cartoons

PAT BAGLEY
Salt Lake Tribune (UT)

JOHN COLE
Scranton Times-Tribune

DARYL CAGLE
MSNBC.COM

LOOK AT ME!!

LOOK AT ME!

DARYL CAGLE MSNBC.com

McCain and the Lobbyist

Minor personal controversy erupted for straight-laced John McCain when allegations surfaced that he had been somehow "inappropriate" with lobbyist Vicki Iseman in the 1990s. The New York Times quoted anonymous McCain aides who said they warned the Arizona senator and Iseman to stay away from each other prior to McCain's 2000 presidential campaign. Nothing much came of the story. Both McCain and Iseman denied any wrongdoing, and any vague accusations of "favoritism" seemed to be lost in the dust on the campaign trail. But nothing makes cartoonists' pens twitter like an unsubstantiated sex scandal.

LOBBYISTS
JOHN McCAIN
HERO IN THE WAR AGAINST LOBBYISTS
HUFFAKER
WWW.CAGLECARTOONS.COM

SANDY HUFFAKER
Cagle Cartoons

MIKE LANE, Cagle Cartoons

JIMMY MARGULIES, The Record (NJ)

BOB ENGLEHART, Hartford Courant

JOHN COLE
Scranton Times-Tribune

BRIAN FAIRRINGTON
Cagle Cartoons

OLLE JOHANSSON
Sweden

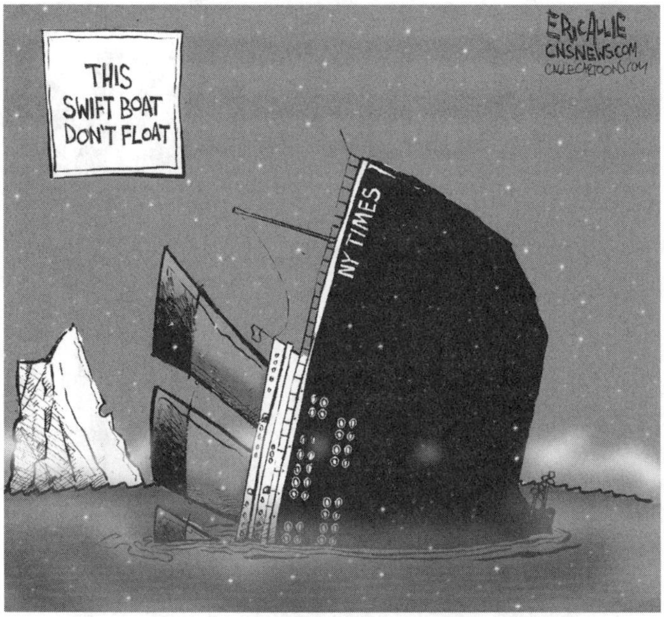

THIS SWIFT BOAT DON'T FLOAT
NY TIMES
ERICALLIE CNSNEWS.COM CAGLECARTOONS.COM

ERIC ALLIE, Politicalcartoons.com

THERE WAS NEVER ANY ROMANCE...
TELL ME ABOUT IT...
LOBBYIST "FRIEND"
ADAM ZYGLIS

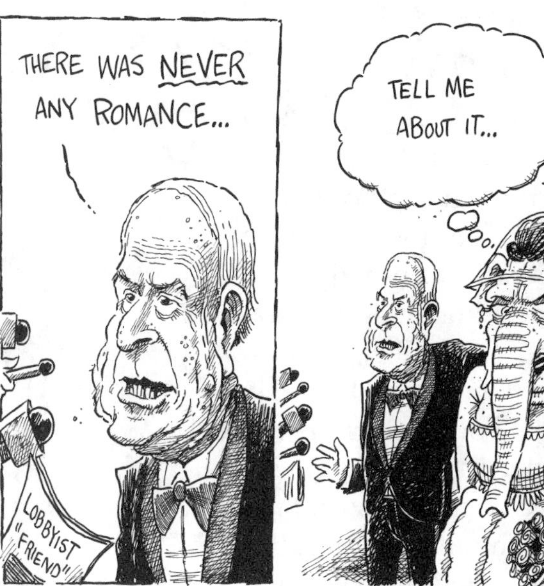

ADAM ZYGLIS, Buffalo News

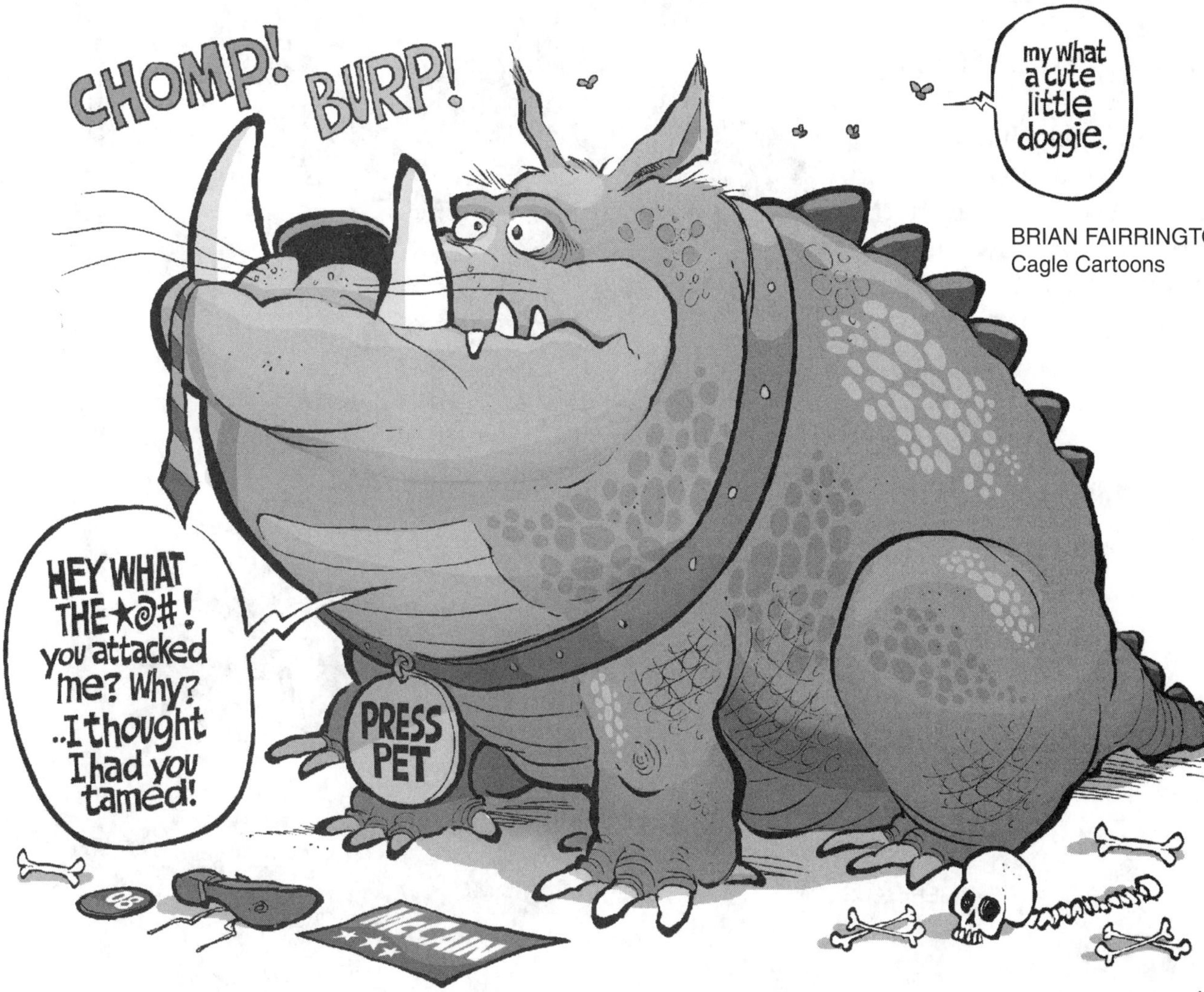

CHOMP! BURP!
my what a cute little doggie.
HEY WHAT THE★@#! you attacked me? Why? ..I thought I had you tamed!
PRESS PET
08
McCAIN

BRIAN FAIRRINGTON
Cagle Cartoons

Hillary vs. Obama

After the other candidates dropped out, the race for the Democratic nomination became a knock-down, drag-out showdown between Hillary Clinton and Barack Obama. For months the two were neck and neck. Their respective camps went back and forth with real numbers and projected numbers of delegates and superdelegates and the popular vote. Ultimately, instead of bringing the Dems together for what many felt should have been a time to rally and take back the White House after the reign of Bush terror, Clinton and Obama threatened to rip the party in two.

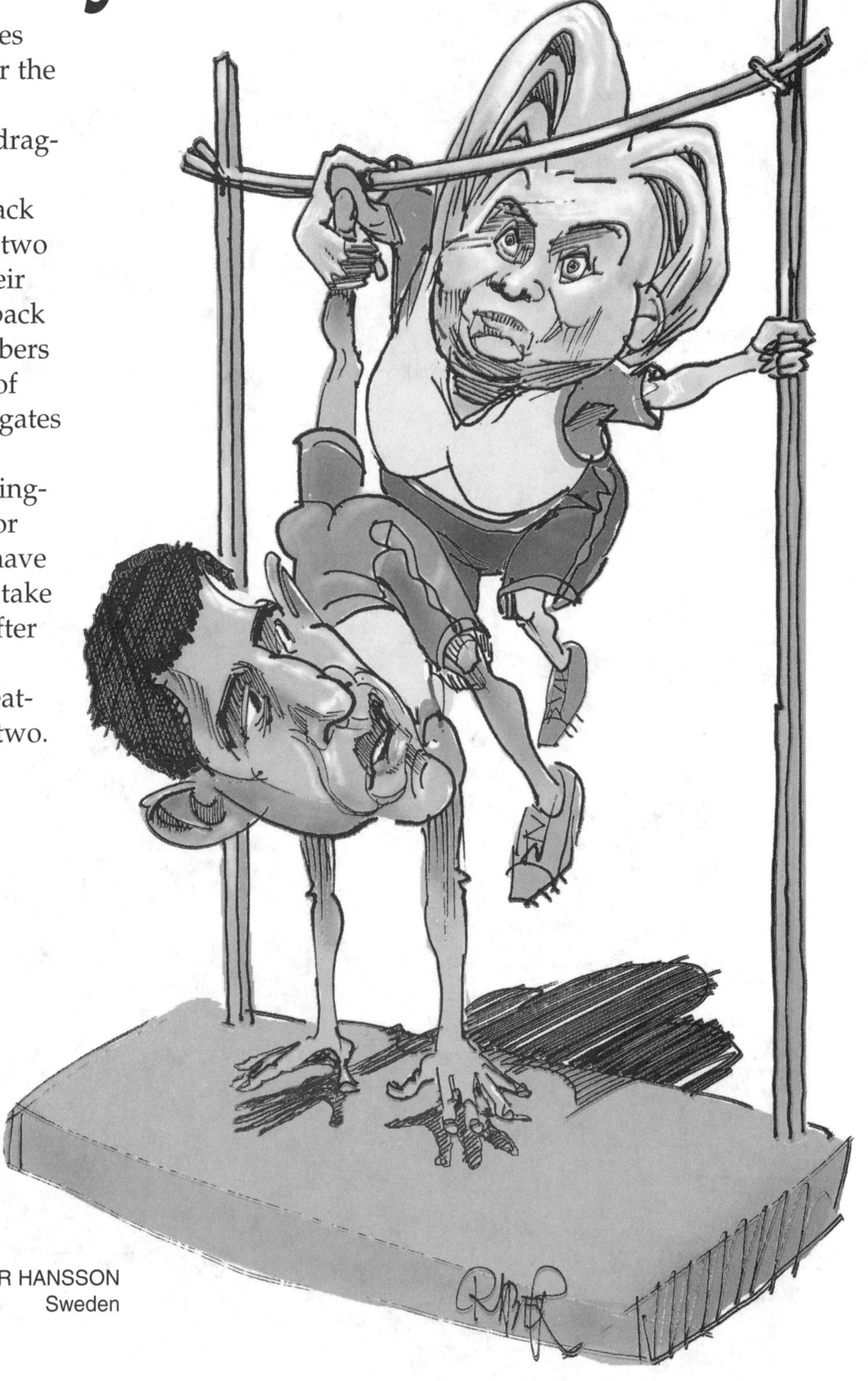

RIBER HANSSON
Sweden

DARYL CAGLE
MSNBC.COM

ADAM ZYGLIS
Buffalo News

CHRISTO KOMARNITSKI, Bulgaria

PATRICK CORRIGAN
Toronto Star

JIMMY MARGULIES
The Record (NJ)

CAMERON CARDOW
Ottawa Citizen
(Canada)

DARYL CAGLE
MSNBC.COM

R.J. MATSON
St. Louis Post Dispatch

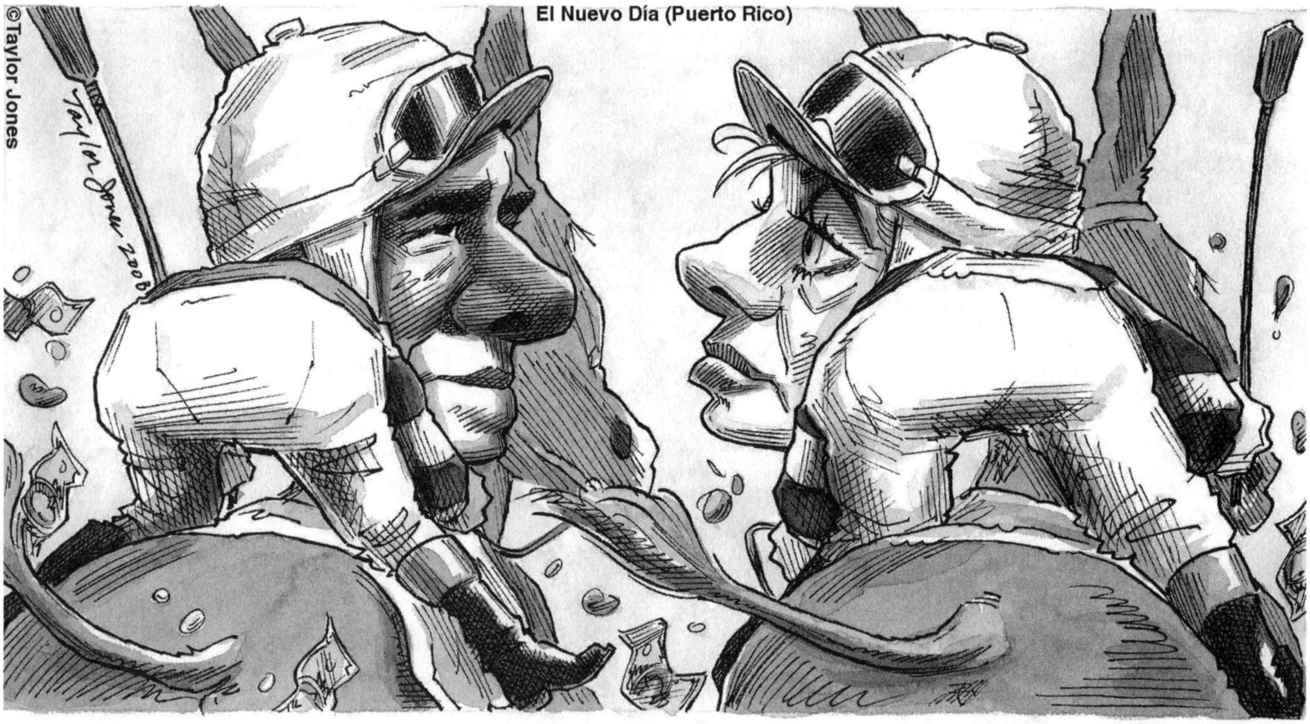

El Nuevo Día (Puerto Rico)

©Taylor Jones

TAYLOR JONES, El Nuevo Dia

If Obama was a state he'd be California Maria Shriver

NIK SCOTT, Australia

" WE CONTINUE TO GO TOE-TO-TOE FOR THIS NOMINATION BUT WE DO SEE EYE-TO-EYE WHEN IT COMES TO ELECTING A DEMOCRATIC PRESIDENT."
HILLARY CLINTON

BOB ENGLEHART, Hartford Courant

J.D. CROWE, Mobile Register

DARYL CAGLE
MSNBC.COM

JIMMY
MARGULIES
The Record
(NJ)

DARYL CAGLE
MSNBC.com

VINCE O'FARRELL, Illawarra Mercury, Australia

JOHN TREVER, Albuquerque Journal

FREDERICK DELIGNE, Nice-Matin, France

THOMAS "TAB" BOLDT, Calgary Sun (Canada)

SANDY HUFFAKER, Cagle Cartoons

MIKE LANE, Cagle Cartoons

IT'S THREE A.M... BUT THERE'S A PHONE IN THE WHITE HOUSE AND IT'S RINGING...
tabtoons@telus.net
Caglecartoons.com
..IT'S OVER, HILLARY. GO TO BED..
Z Z Z
3:00

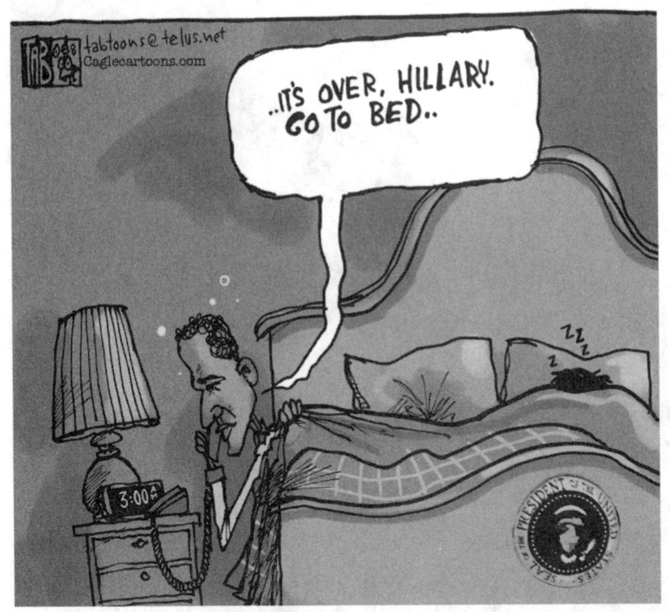

THOMAS "TAB" BOLDT, Calgary Sun (Canada)

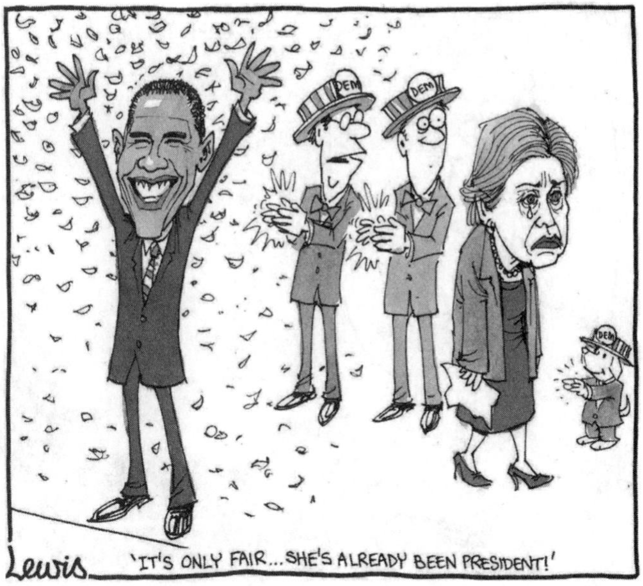

DEM
DEM
DEM
Lewis
'IT'S ONLY FAIR... SHE'S ALREADY BEEN PRESIDENT!'

PETER LEWIS, Newcastle Herald Australia

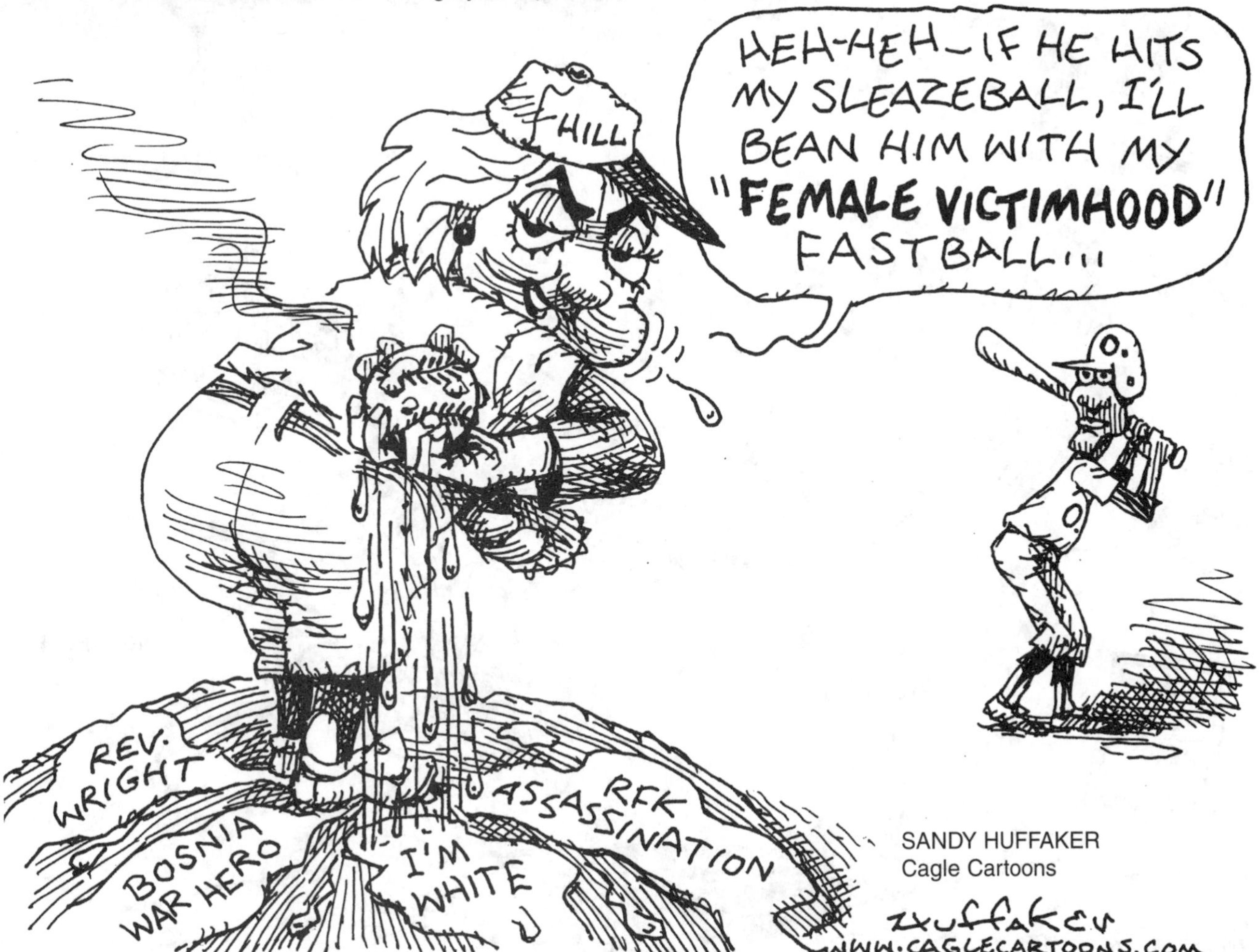

HEH-HEH - IF HE HITS MY SLEAZEBALL, I'LL BEAN HIM WITH MY "FEMALE VICTIMHOOD" FASTBALL...
HILL
REV. WRIGHT
BOSNIA WAR HERO
I'M WHITE
RFK ASSASSINATION
Huffaker
WWW.CAGLECARTOONS.COM

SANDY HUFFAKER
Cagle Cartoons

PAT BAGLEY
Salt Lake Tribune (UT)

MIKE KEEFE
Denver Post

OLLE JOHANSSON
Sweden

ANTONIO NERILICON, Mexico

Hillary Under Fire

In a press conference on the campaign trail, Hillary Clinton told a rapt crowd about her visit as first lady to war-torn Yugoslavia in 1996, where she had to run from sniper bullets. The anecdote was meant to cast Hillary as having been a thick-skinned foreign policy adviser in hubby Bill's administration.

Unfortunately for Hillary, CBS dug up footage and the snipers were nowhere to be found; there was just the first lady and teenage Chelsea Clinton sauntering casually across the tarmac from their plane for a smiling meet-and-greet with the locals. That was, of course, when Hillary actually came under fire.

DARYL CAGLE
MSNBC.COM

OLLE JOHANSSON, Sweden

ERIC ALLIE
Politicalcartoons.com

MIKE KEEFE
Denver Post

JIMMY MARGULIES, The Record (NJ)

SANDY HUFFAKER, Cagle Cartoons

GARY McCOY, Cagle Cartoons

PAT BAGLEY, Salt Lake Tribune (UT)

R.J. MATSON
St. Louis Post Dispatch

NATE BEELER, Washington Examiner

SANDY HUFFAKER
Cagle Cartoons

JOE HELLER, Green Bay Press Gazette

ERIC ALLIE
Politicalcartoons.com

JOHN COLE
Scranton
Times-Tribune

MONTE
WOLVERTON
Cagle Cartoons

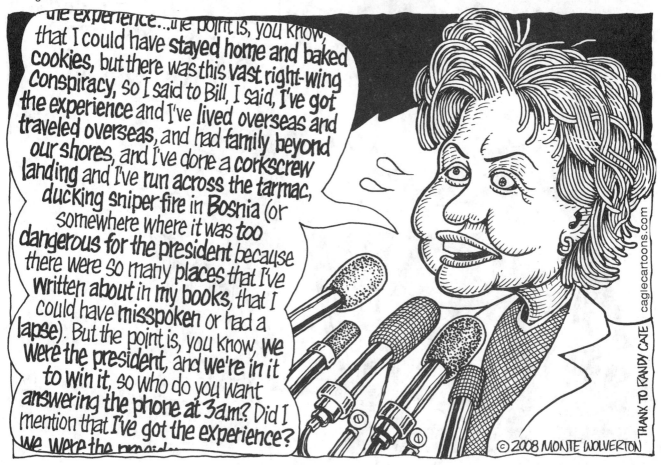

Obama's "Bitter" Words

In the midst of his snowballing momentum rolling into the November election, Barack Obama seriously tripped up when he let slip some comments about economically frustrated small-town Americans, who "get bitter and cling to guns or religion." No amount of backpedaling could undo the damage. The media had been looking for a gap in his armor, and they were all too happy to hit "elitist and divisive" Ivy League, big-city Obama's Achilles heel. These bitter words haunted Obama the rest of the way down the campaign trail.

And he might as well have drawn a target on himself for all those pen-totin' cartoonists.

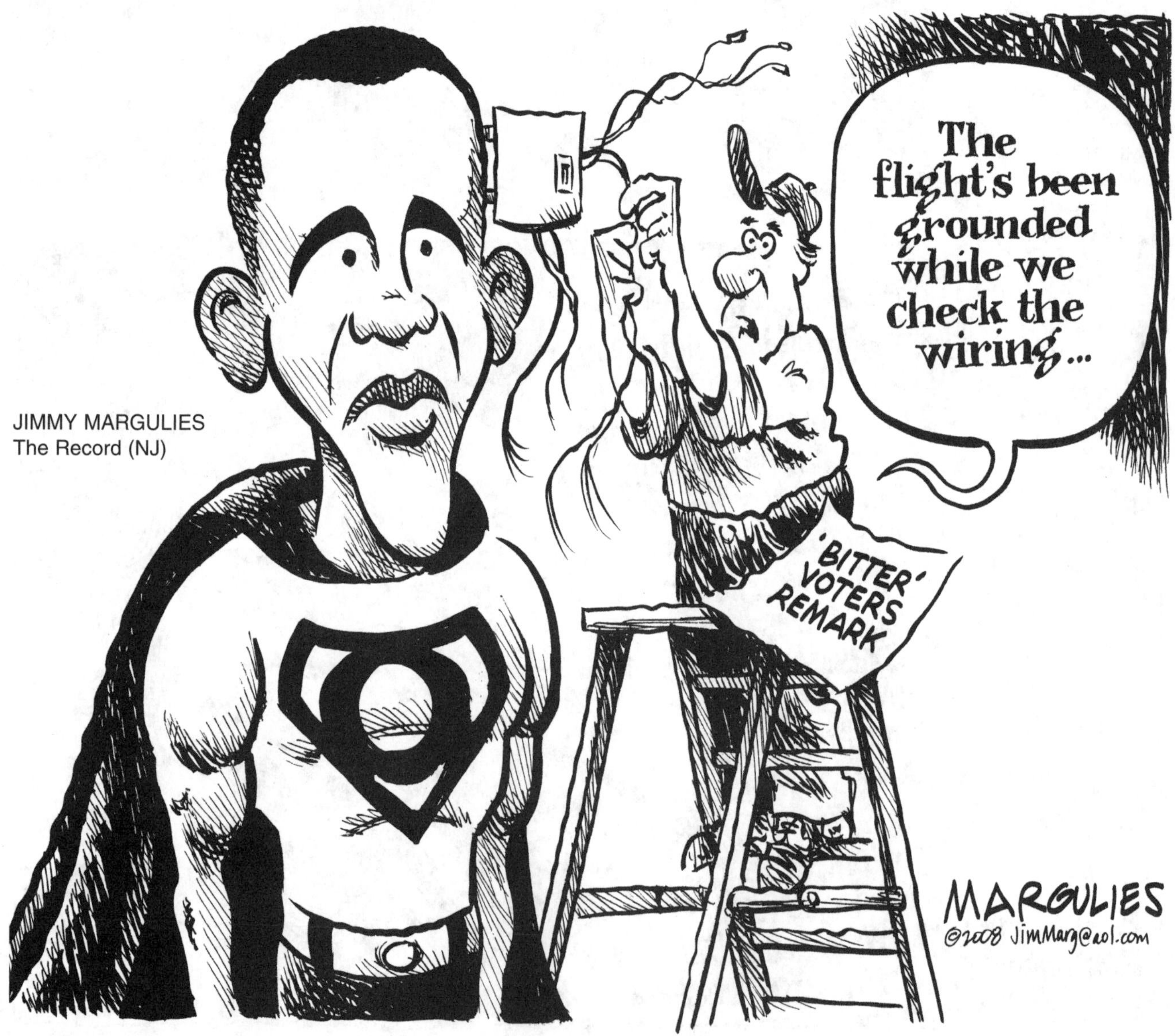

JIMMY MARGULIES
The Record (NJ)

THEY WERE ANGRY AND BITTER AND THEY THOUGHT THEY'D TEACH THAT YOUNG ELITIST A LESSON.

PENNSYLVANIA

Obama '08

DELIVERANCE

BARACK OBAMA

HILLARY AND BILL CLINTON

R.J. MATSON, Roll Call

© 4/15/08 HARTFORD COURANT
"BITTER" "CLING TO"
caglecartoons.com
courant.com/boblog
BOB ENGLEHART
Hartford Courant

NEWS
OBAMA BELITTLES WITH 'BITTER' REMARK
OBAMA FOR PRESIDENT
THEY'RE TRYING TO MAKE A MOUNTAIN OUT OF A MOLEHILL
UNITER JUDGEMENT LEADERSHIP
CAGLECARTOONS.COM
ERIC ALLIE
Cagle Cartoons

JOHN COLE
Scranton Times-Tribune

NATE BEELER
Washington Examiner

BRIAN FAIRRINGTON
Cagle Cartoons

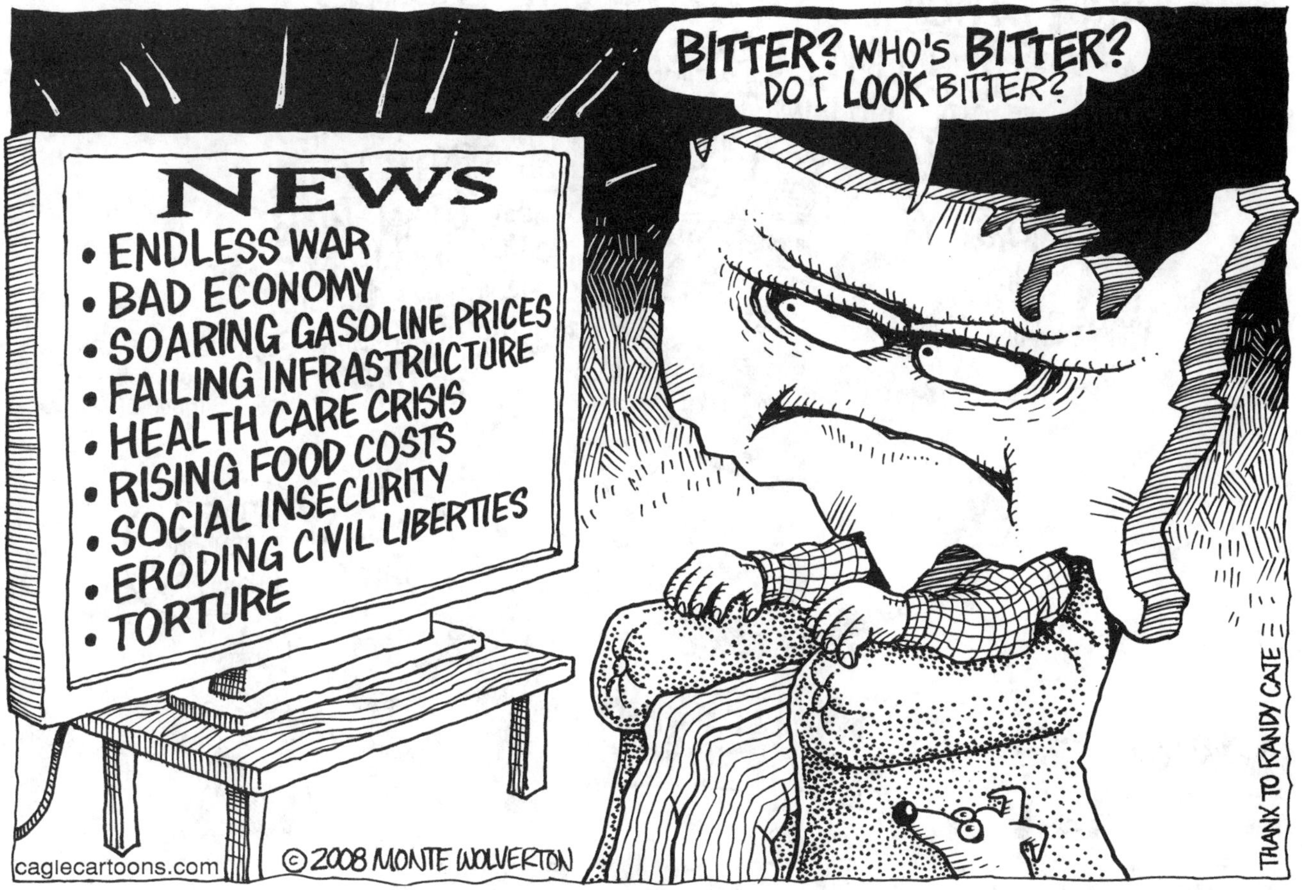

BITTER? WHO'S BITTER? DO I LOOK BITTER?

NEWS
• ENDLESS WAR
• BAD ECONOMY
• SOARING GASOLINE PRICES
• FAILING INFRASTRUCTURE
• HEALTH CARE CRISIS
• RISING FOOD COSTS
• SOCIAL INSECURITY
• ERODING CIVIL LIBERTIES
• TORTURE

caglecartoons.com
© 2008 MONTE WOLVERTON
THANX TO RANDY CATE

MONTE WOLVERTON
Cagle Cartoons

DARYL CAGLE
MSNBC.COM

JOHN DARKOW
Columbia Daily
Tribune (MO)

GARY MCCOY
Cagle Cartoons

PAT BAGLEY, Salt Lake Tribune

MIKE KEEFE, Denver Post

ADAM ZYGLIS
Buffalo News

The Dropouts

Every dusty presidential campaign trail is riddled with the dried-out husks of failed campaigns set asunder. This year, though, we saw some more spectacular deaths. Sometimes they were quick and blindsiding, such as Joe Biden's bumbling "racist" Obama comments. Others were kind of predictable, as in Dennis Kucinich's alleged U.F.O. sighting; and others are just sad (see: Mike Huckabee's long, slow slip to the side of the road).

Of course cartoonists delighted in their awkward falls from the party platform.

TAYLOR JONES
Politicalcartoons.com

R.J. MATSON, Roll Call

BOB ENGLEHART
Hartford Courant

MIKE KEEFE
Denver Post

BRIAN FAIRRINGTON
Cagle Cartoons

SANDY HUFFAKER, Cagle Cartoons

GARY MCCOY
Cagle Cartoons

J.D. CROWE
Mobile Register

JOHN TREVER
Albuquerque Journal

JOHN COLE
Scranton Times-Tribune

HUCKABEE
DELEGATES
caglecartoons.com
©MATSON ROLL CALL
"IT'S MATHEMATICALLY IMPOSSIBLE FOR SO FEW CHOCOLATES TO TASTE SOOO GOOD!"
Taylor Jones 2008
©Taylor Jones
The Devil made me do it...
amen Brother.
Spit on MITT
LDS
HATE in 08
GOP GOD
E van GELS
VOTE
JESUS 2008
MORMONS are the NEW JEWS
HUCKABEE'S Anti-MORMON Rhetoric

R.J. MATSON, Roll Call

TAYLOR JONES
Politicalcartoons.com

BRIAN FAIRRINGTON
Cagle Cartoons

ADAM ZYGLIS
Buffalo News

JUST LIKE EVOLUTION, 'ARITHMETIC' IS SCIENTIFIC MUMBO JUMBO...
DELEGATE MATH
2380
-1346
1034
REMAIN
1191
-217
974
I NEED
THEREFORE:
McCAIN WILL
WIN
HUCK 2008
MIRACLES

POLITICIAN TALENTS
PLAYS THE BASS
PLAYS THE SAX
PLAYS THE VICTIM
MEDIA HATES ME
HUCKABEE
BILL
HILLARY

GARY MCCOY, Cagle Cartoons

RISE! TAKE UP YOUR BED AND WALK! C'MON! I MAJORED IN MIRACLES!
HUCK CAMPAIGN

BOB ENGLEHART, Hartford Courant

IDENTIFY THE REAL MIRACLE:
A WATER BECOMES WINE...

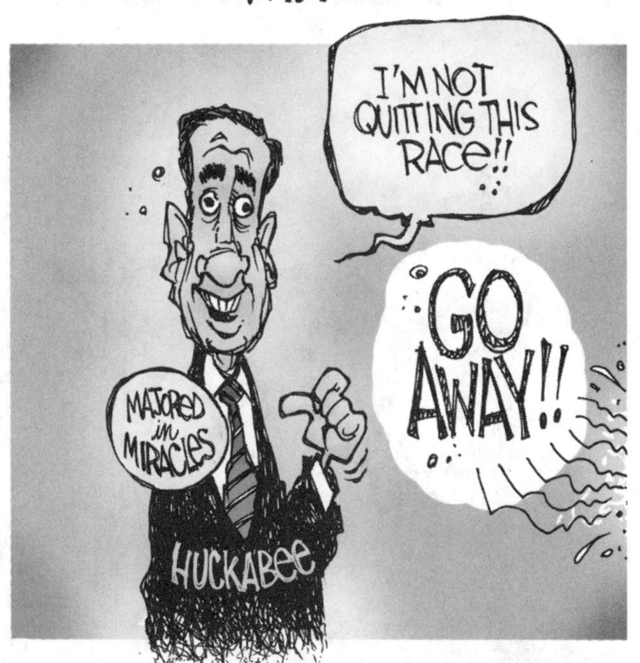
I'M NOT QUITTING THIS RACE!!
GO AWAY!!
MAJORED in MIRACLES
HUCKABEE
B "15 MINUTES" BECOMES 15 MONTHS...
JOHN COLE THE TIMES-TRIBUNE/SCRANTON, PA

JOHN COLE, Scranton Times-Tribune

TAYLOR JONES
El Nuevo Dia

SANDY HUFFAKER, Cagle Cartoons

J.D. CROWE, Mobile Register

JOHN COLE
Scranton Times-Tribune

JOHN TREVER, Albuquerque Journal

JOHN TREVER, Albuquerque Journal

JOHN TREVER, Albuquerque Journal

JOHN TREVER, Albuquerque Journal

Clintons Attack

Former President Bill Clinton was the pink-faced elephant in the room from the start of his wife's presidential campaign. A vote for Hillary was also a vote for First Lady Bill, who seemed to be attached to her hip (or perhaps at the end of her leash). Everyone presumed having a popular ex-president for a husband would, of course, help Hillary Clinton but that was before Bill opened his mouth out on the campaign trail. Bill was combative with the media and civilians in inteviews, and he went far out on a limb in his harsh and often racially charged criticisms of Barack Obama. Often the criticisms of Hillary's campaign had more to do with big-mouthed Bill than with herself.

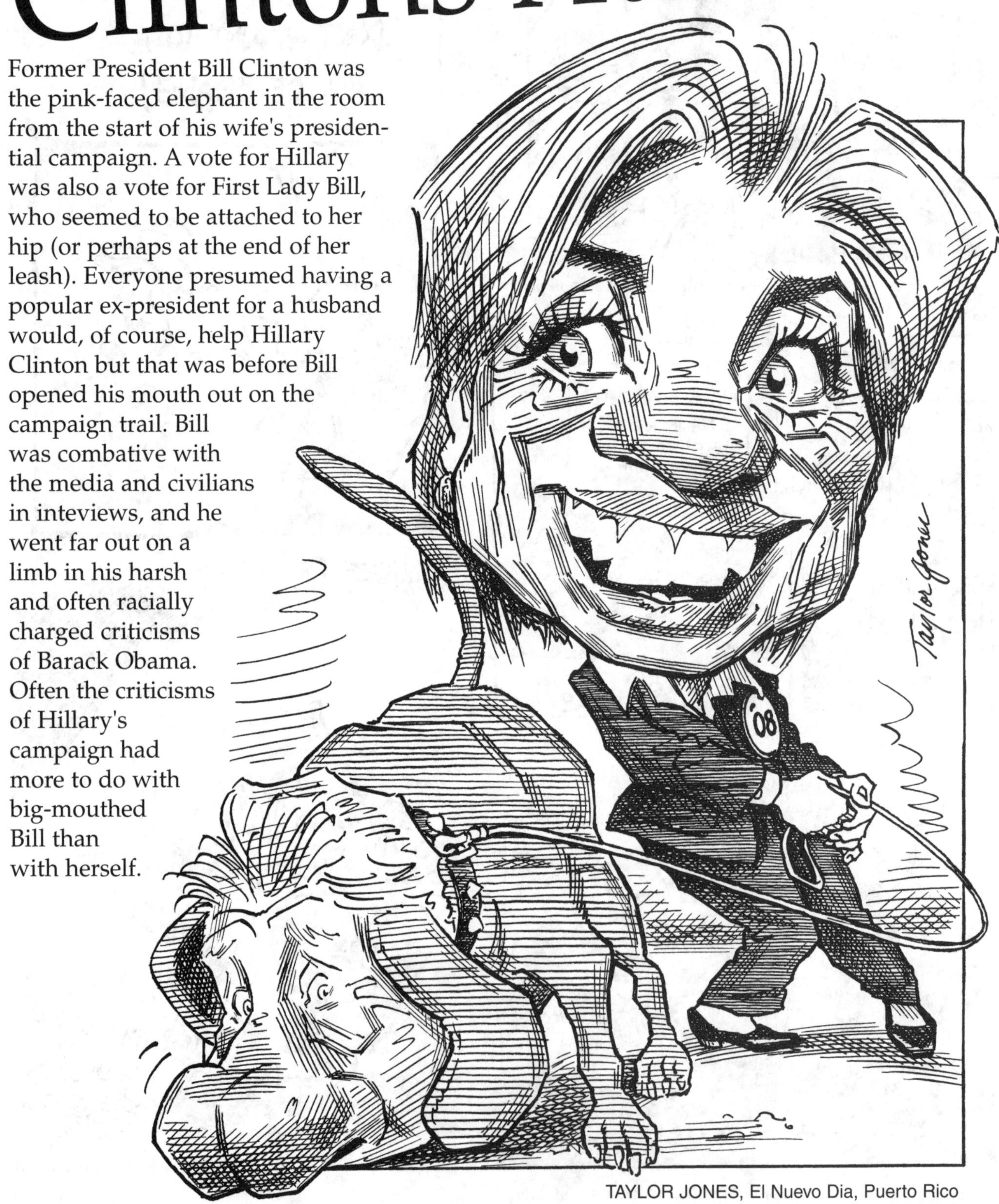

TAYLOR JONES, El Nuevo Dia, Puerto Rico

DARYL CAGLE, MSNBC.COM

PAT BAGLEY
Salt Lake Tribune (UT)

ADAM ZYGLIS, Buffalo News

NATE BEELER, Washington Examiner

JIMMY MARGULIES
The Record (NJ)

ERIC ALLIE
Politicalcartoons.com

GARY MCCOY, Cagle Cartoons

MICHAEL MCPARLANE, Politicalcartoons.com

ERIC ALLIE, Politicalcartoons.com

R.J. MATSON, St. Louis Post Dispatch

NATE BEELER, Washington Examiner

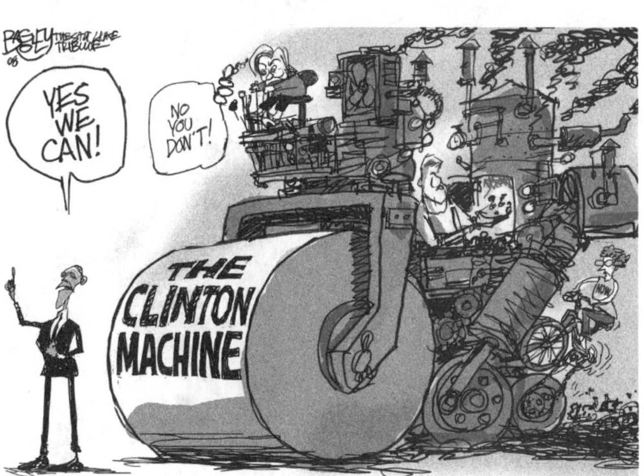

PAT BAGLEY, Salt Lake Tribune (UT)

MIKE LANE, Cagle Cartoons

NATE BEELER
Washington Examiner

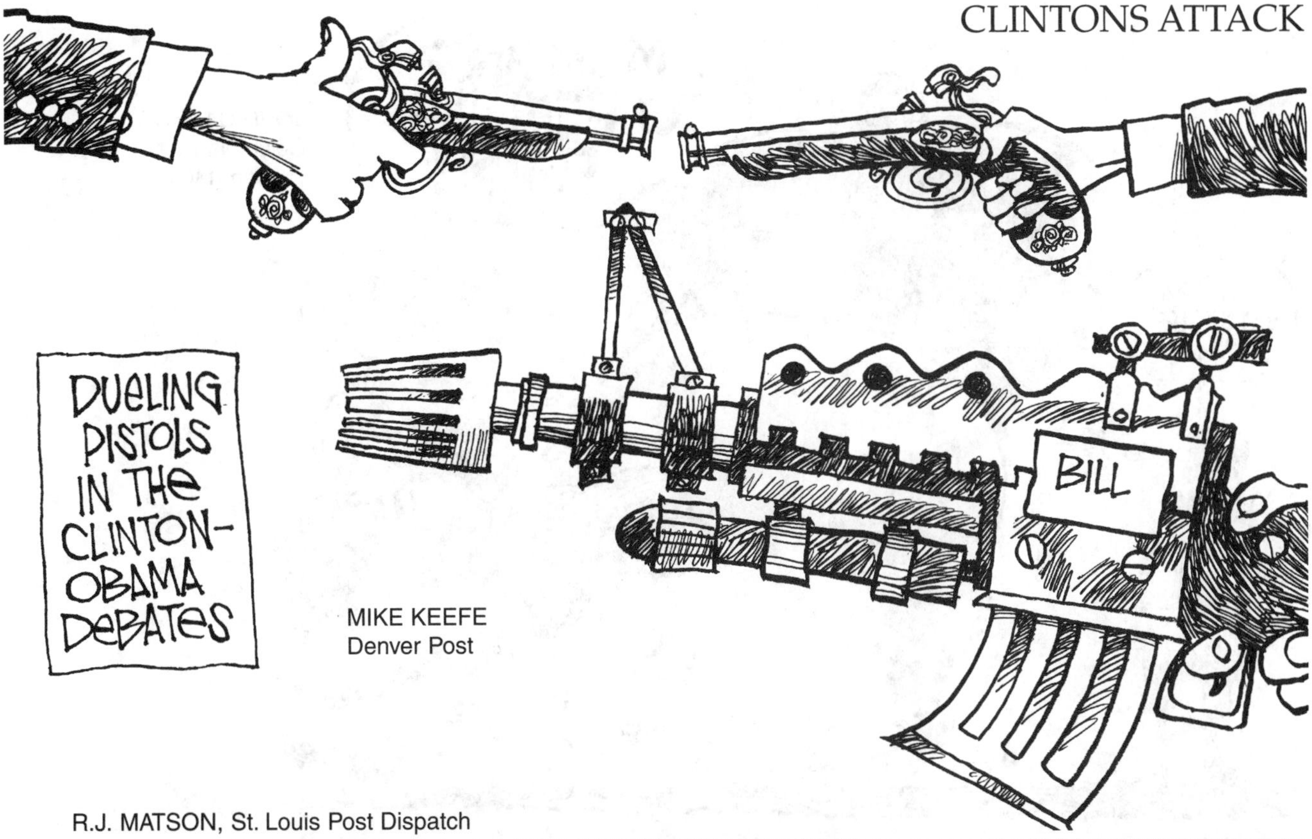

DUELING PISTOLS IN THE CLINTON-OBAMA DEBATES

BILL

MIKE KEEFE
Denver Post

R.J. MATSON, St. Louis Post Dispatch

THE TORCH HAS BEEN PASSED TO A NEW GENERATION

CHANGE

OBAMA

OBAMA

Obama

'08

NEVER TRUST ANYONE OVER 70

OR UNDER 50

Obama

©MATSON
caglecartoons.com
ST. LOUIS POST-DISPATCH

"WHAT A BUNCH OF HAS-BEENS AND WANNA-BEES!"

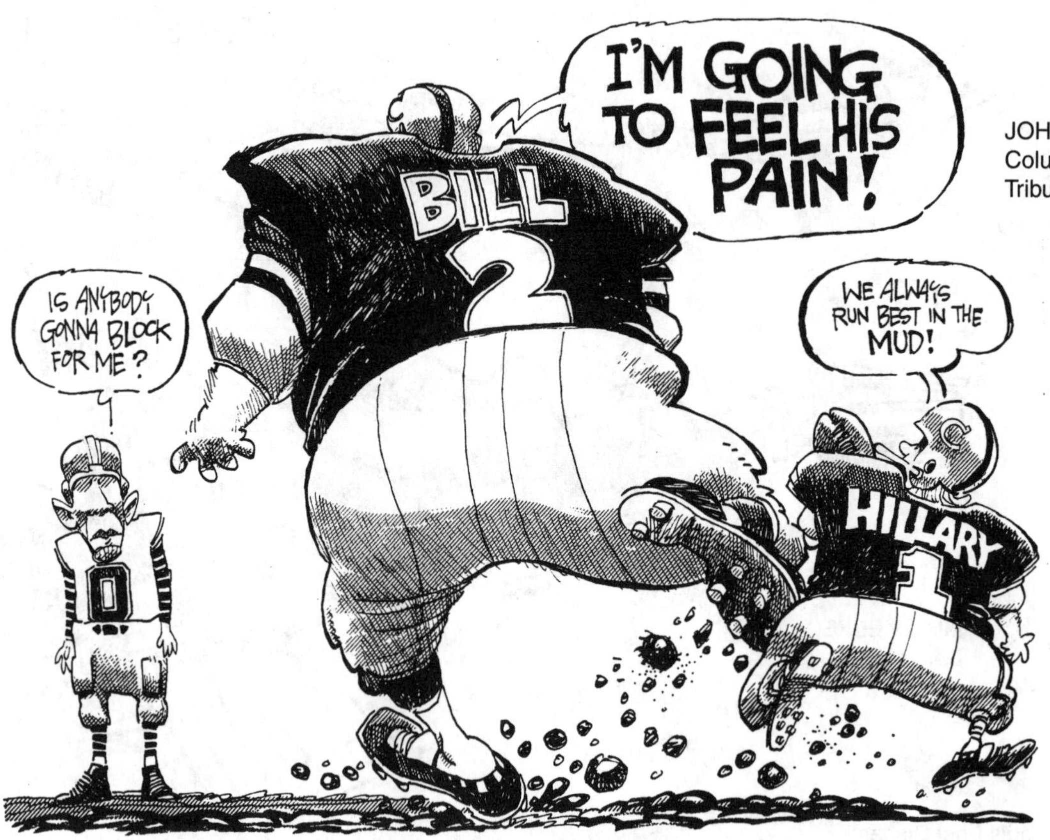

I'M GOING TO FEEL HIS PAIN!

BILL 2

IS ANYBODY GONNA BLOCK FOR ME?

WE ALWAYS RUN BEST IN THE MUD!

HILLARY 1

0

JOHN DARKOW
Columbia Daily
Tribune (MO)

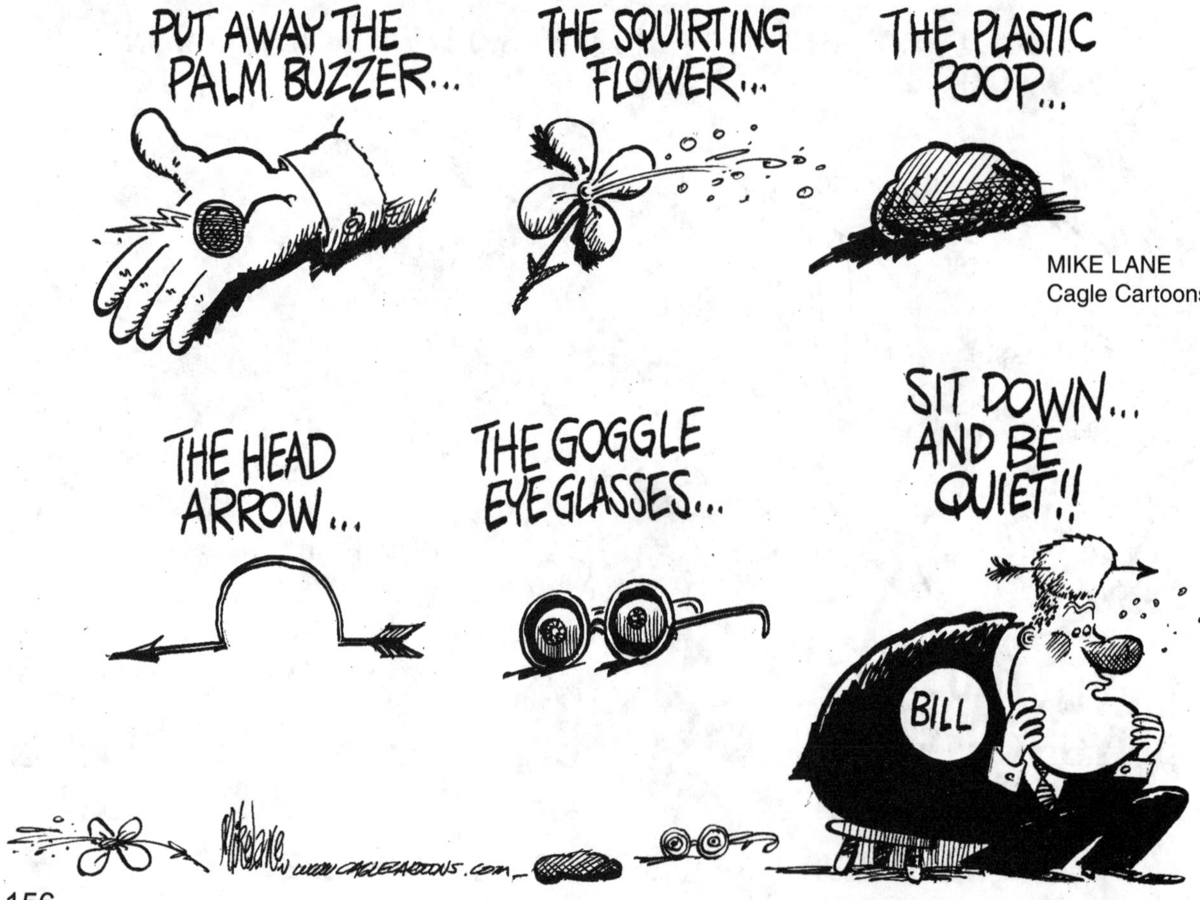

THE SQUIRTING FLOWER...

THE PLASTIC POOP...

MIKE LANE
Cagle Cartoons

THE HEAD ARROW...

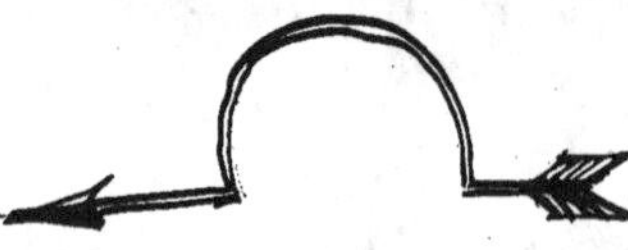

THE GOGGLE EYE GLASSES...

SIT DOWN... AND BE QUIET!!

CHAPPATTE
Int'l Herald Tribune

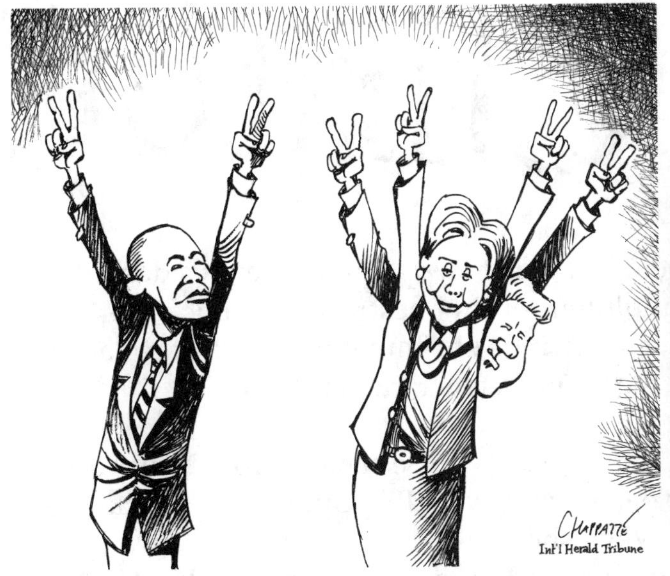

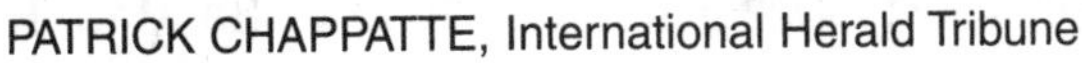

PATRICK CHAPPATTE, International Herald Tribune

©OLLE08 WWW.TECKNAR-OLLE.SE
HONEY I TOLD YOU BOXING IS NOT A TEAM SPORT...
OBAMA
SOUTH CAROLINA

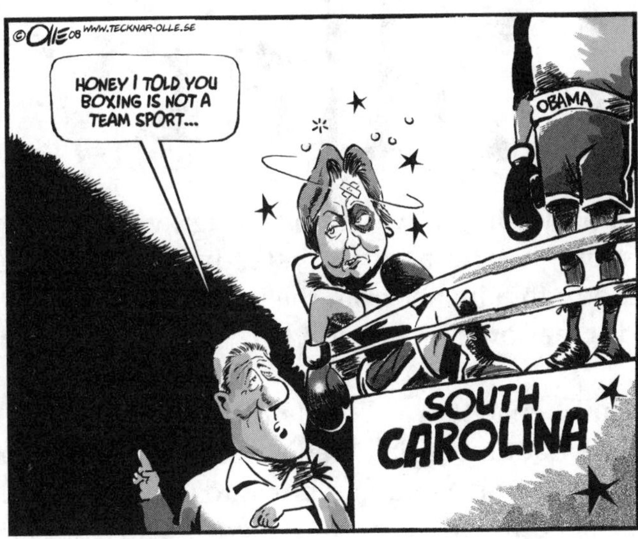

OLLE JOHANSSON, Sweden

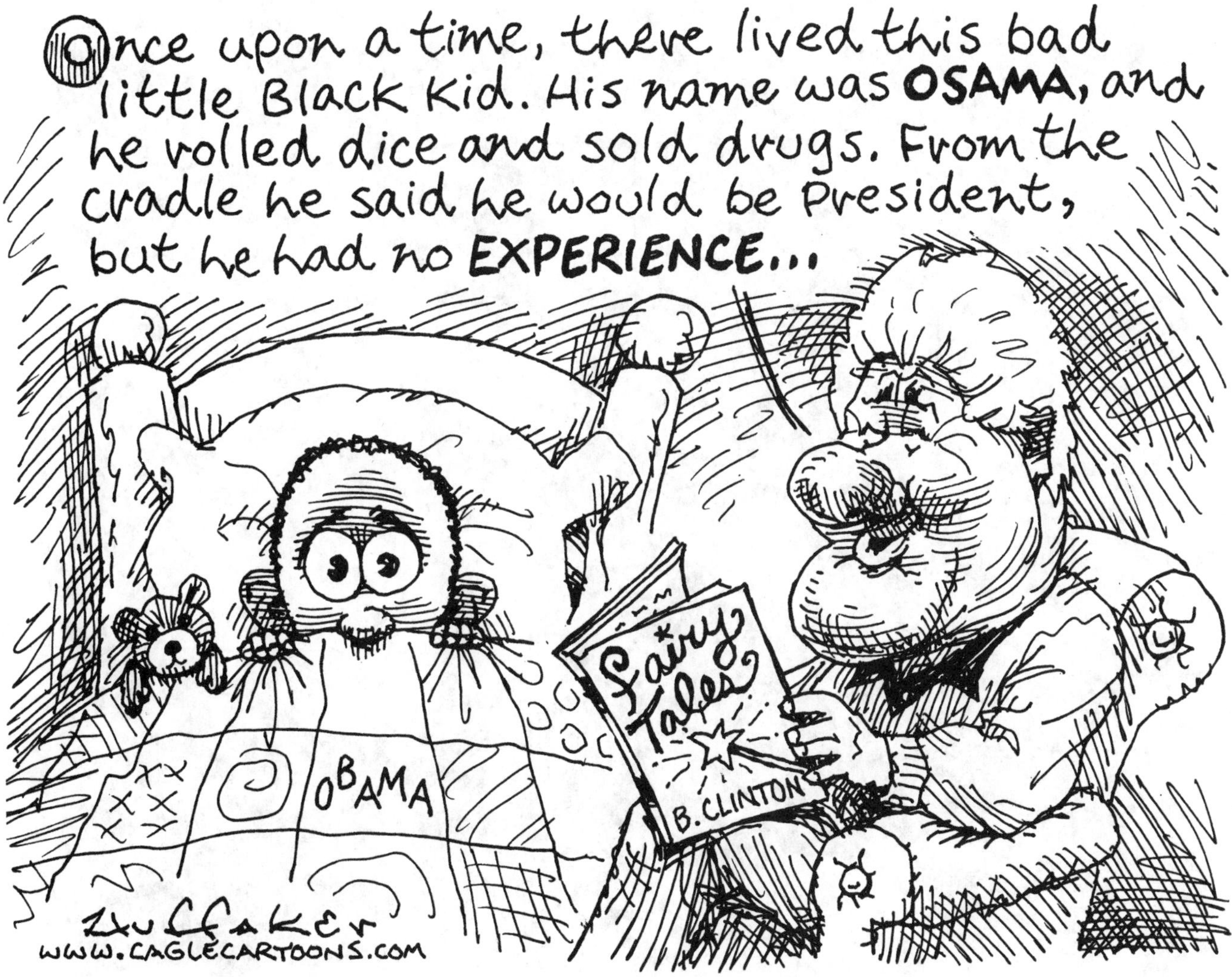

Once upon a time, there lived this bad little Black Kid. His name was OSAMA, and he rolled dice and sold drugs. From the cradle he said he would be President, but he had no EXPERIENCE...
Fairy Tales
B. CLINTON
OBAMA
HUFFAKER
WWW.CAGLECARTOONS.COM

SANDY HUFFAKER, Cagle Cartoons

Hillary Clinton

Hillary Clinton was a polarizing figure since before she first stepped into the presidential spotlight. Her reign as first lady had been a tumultuous one (at best), and America was ready to hate her from the get-go (even if they felt a twinge of sympathy, too). But Hillary dug her own grave with her "shrill" attacks on the other Democratic candidates.

Hill's tenacity was both her key to success and her tragic flaw. The senator from New York took a lot more flak than she might have if her name were, well, Bill. But Hillary's bark was always worse than her bite into Obama's lead. When she finally gave up the gun, cartoonists had to wonder: was America really not ready for a lady president, or was Hillary just one woman – with a personality too big for the Oval Office?

PETER LEWIS
Newcastle Herald Australia

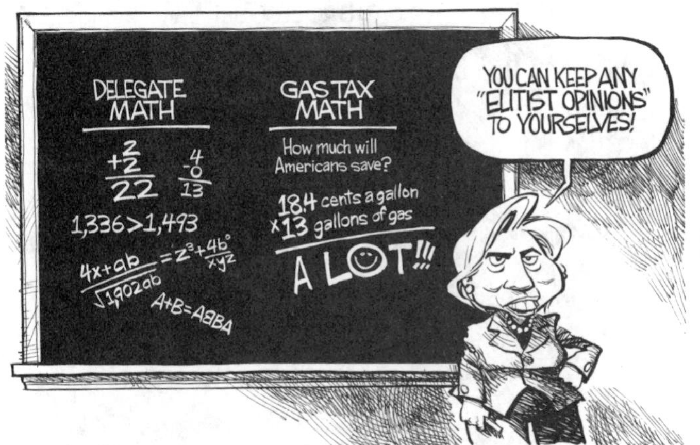

NATE BEELER, Washington Examiner

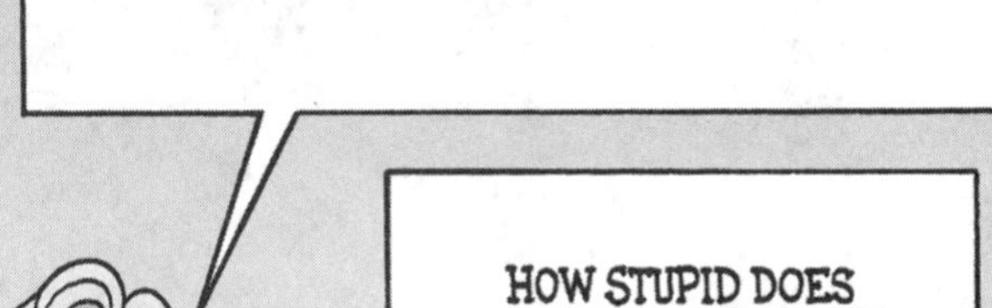

R.J. MATSON, Roll Call

JOHN COLE, Scranton Times-Tribune

ADAM ZYGLIS, Buffalo News

ERIC ALLIE
Cagle Cartoons

MIKE KEEFE, Denver Post

PAT BAGLEY, Salt Lake Tribune (UT)

JIMMY MARGULIES, The Record (NJ)

PAT BAGLEY, Salt Lake Tribune (UT)

NATE BEELER, Washington Examiner

JOHN COLE, Scranton Times-Tribune

JOHN COLE
Scranton Times-Tribune

GARY MCCOY, Cagle Cartoons

DAVID FITZSIMMONS, Arizona Daily Star

HILLARY RODHAM = THE EARLY YEARS

JOHN DARKOW, Columbia Daily Tribune (MO)

JIMMY MARGULIES, The Record (NJ)

STUBBORN AS A...

R.J. MATSON, St. Louis Post Dispatch

TERRY "AISLIN" MOSHER, Montreal Gazette

DWAYNE BOOTH, Mr. Fish

CAMERON CARDOW, Ottawa Citizen (Canada)

HILLARY'S LAST STAND

PETAR PISMESTROVIC, Austria

VINCE O'FARRELL
Illawarra Mercury, Australia

JIMMY MARGULIES
The Record (NJ)

DARYL CAGLE
MSNBC.COM

ONWARD MARCH!
(actually it's almost May)

How long is this thing?
Is there any end in sight?
Does anyone have any scissors?
hey look- BILL is riding her Coattails...

BRIAN FAIRRINGTON
Cagle Cartoons

NOW I'VE GOT YOU WHERE I WANT YOU! BWA-HA-HA-CACKLE-HA-HA-HA

SANDY HUFFAKER, Cagle Cartoons

I DON'T CARE HOW MUCH IT'S HURTING! THERE'LL BE NO EUTHANIZING TILL AFTER WE'VE WON THE RACE!
HILLARY CAMPAIGN

LARRY WRIGHT, Detroit News

THE HILLARY CAMPAIGN MARCHES ON

J.D. CROWE, Mobile Register

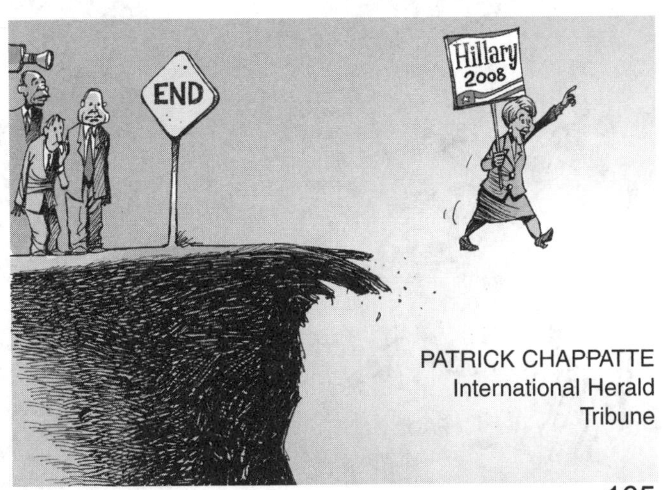
END
Hillary
2008

PATRICK CHAPPATTE
International Herald
Tribune

SHE JUST KEEPS
RUNNING
AND
RUNNING
AND
RUNNING
AND
RUNNING
AND
RUNNING
AND

Hillary

PAT BAGLEY
Salt Lake Tribune (UT)

PAUL ZANETTI
Australia

ADAM ZYGLIS
Buffalo News

NIK SCOTT
Australia

NATE BEELER, Washington Examiner

Hillary

WHAT BUMP?

BROELMAN

PETER BROELMAN, Australia

BOB ENGLEHART
Hartford Courant

caglecartoons.com courant.com/boblog

"That's all Folks!"

BUT I STILL WON THE POPULAR VOTE!!

'08

©2008 CAGLECARTOONS THEBUFFALONEWS

ADAM ZYGLIS

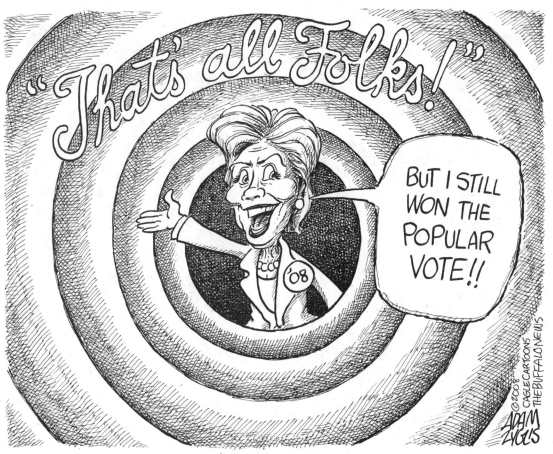

ADAM ZYGLIS
Buffalo News

LOONEY...

PAT BAGLEY
Salt Lake
Tribune

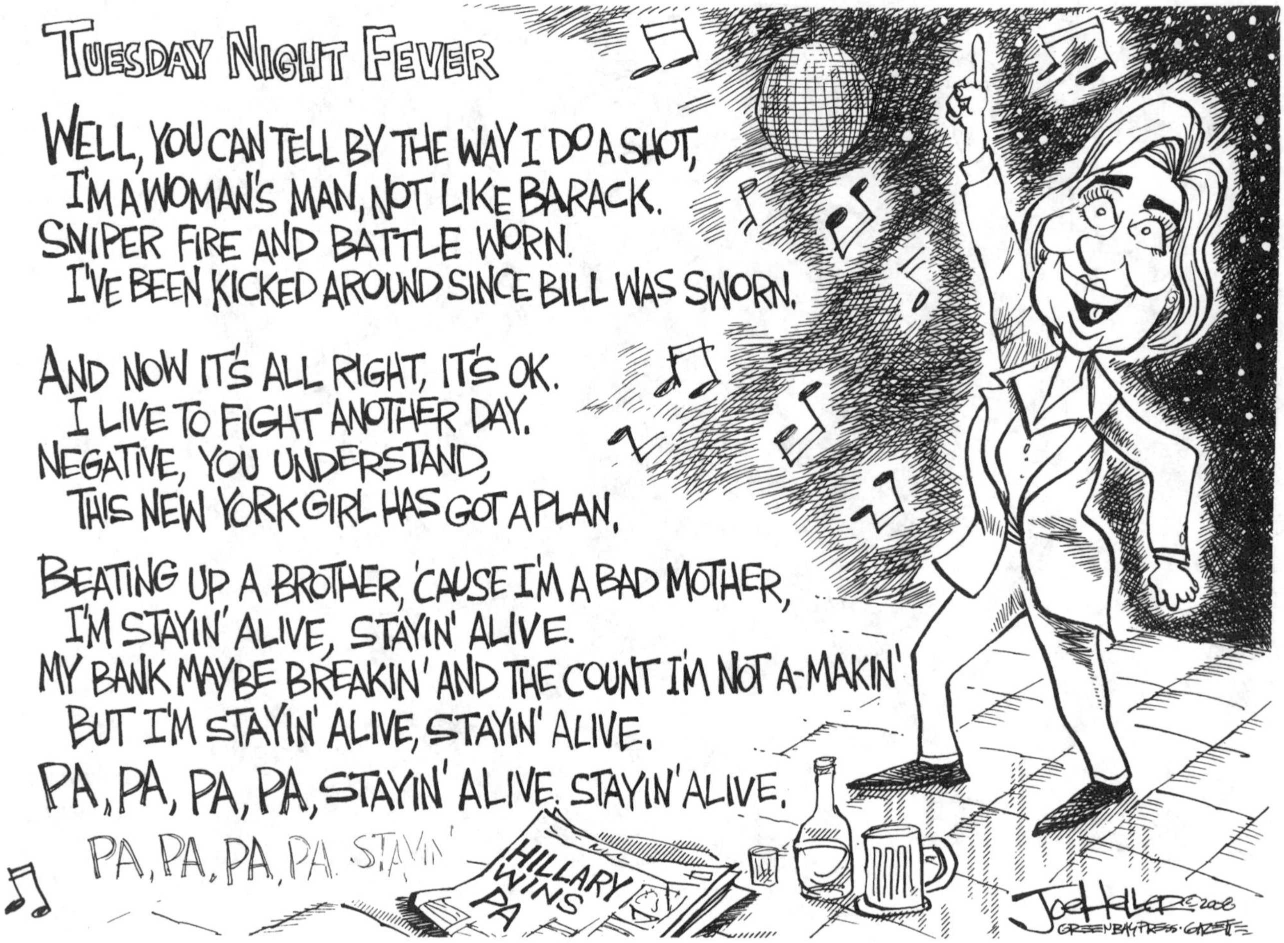

TUESDAY NIGHT FEVER
WELL, YOU CAN TELL BY THE WAY I DO A SHOT,
I'M A WOMAN'S MAN, NOT LIKE BARACK.
SNIPER FIRE AND BATTLE WORN.
I'VE BEEN KICKED AROUND SINCE BILL WAS SWORN.
AND NOW IT'S ALL RIGHT, IT'S OK.
I LIVE TO FIGHT ANOTHER DAY.
NEGATIVE, YOU UNDERSTAND,
THIS NEW YORK GIRL HAS GOT A PLAN.
BEATING UP A BROTHER, 'CAUSE I'M A BAD MOTHER,
I'M STAYIN' ALIVE, STAYIN' ALIVE.
MY BANK MAYBE BREAKIN' AND THE COUNT I'M NOT A-MAKIN'
BUT I'M STAYIN' ALIVE, STAYIN' ALIVE.
PA, PA, PA, PA, STAYIN' ALIVE, STAYIN' ALIVE.
PA, PA, PA, PA, STAYIN'
HILLARY WINS PA
JOE HELLER ©2008 GREEN BAY PRESS-GAZETTE

JOE HELLER, Green Bay Press-Gazette

M. e. COHEN, Politicalcartoons.com

A GAS TAX HOLIDAY IN EVERY TANK!
M.e. COHEN
Humorink.com

ATTACK OF THE 50 FT. WOMAN
THE SALT LAKE TRIBUNE
I LOVE THE LITTLE PEOPLE!
WELCOME TO smallville
population: tiny

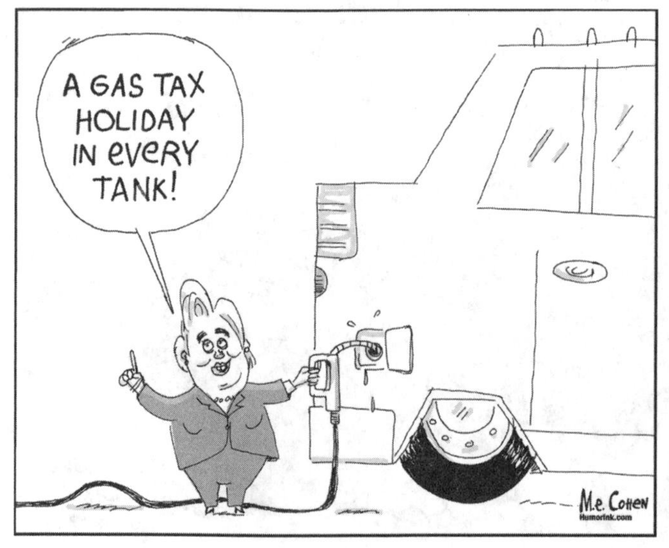

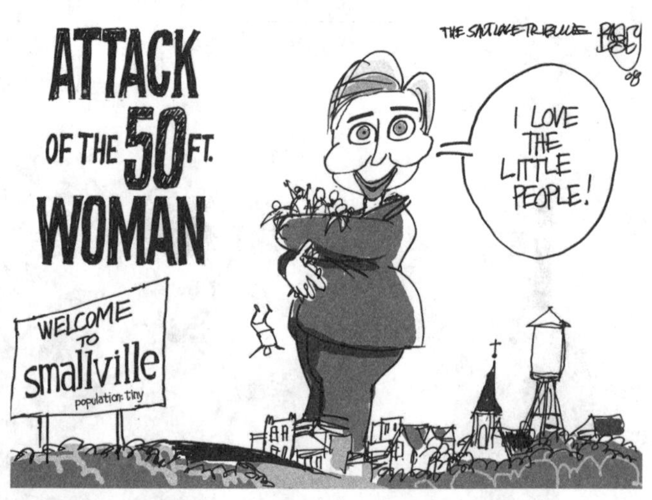

PAT BAGLEY, Salt Lake Tribune

ANOTHER PANDERING, SELF-SERVING SEQUEL...
INDIANA JANE
AND THE GAS CRUSADE!
TAX '08
OPENS MAY 6TH
©2008 CAGLECARTOONS.COM THEBUFFALONEWS
ADAM ZYGLIS

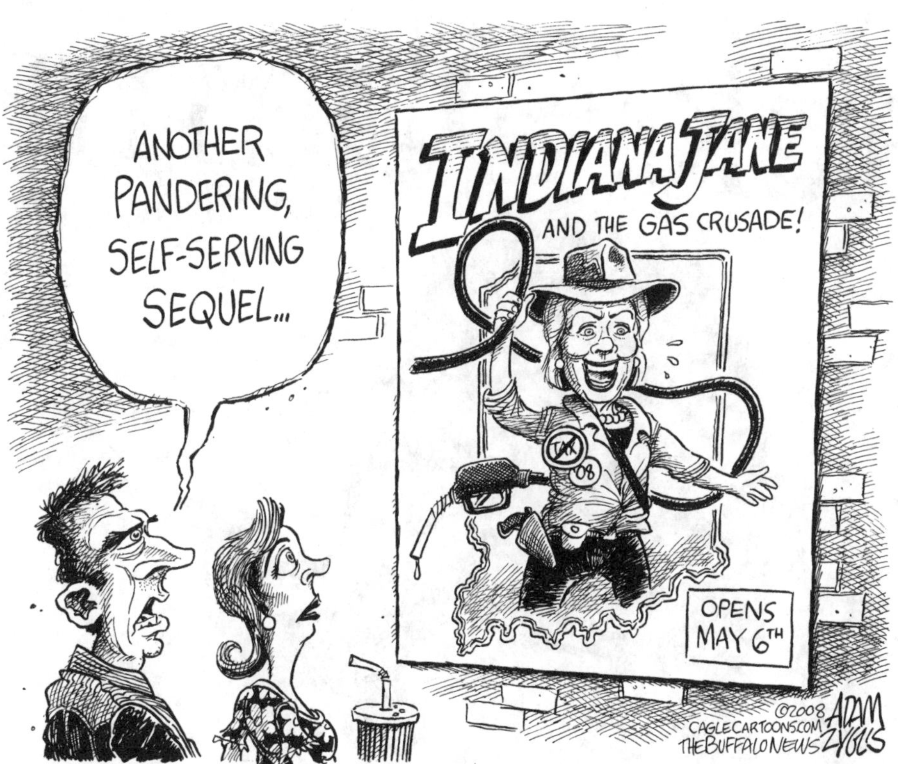

ADAM ZYGLIS
Buffalo News

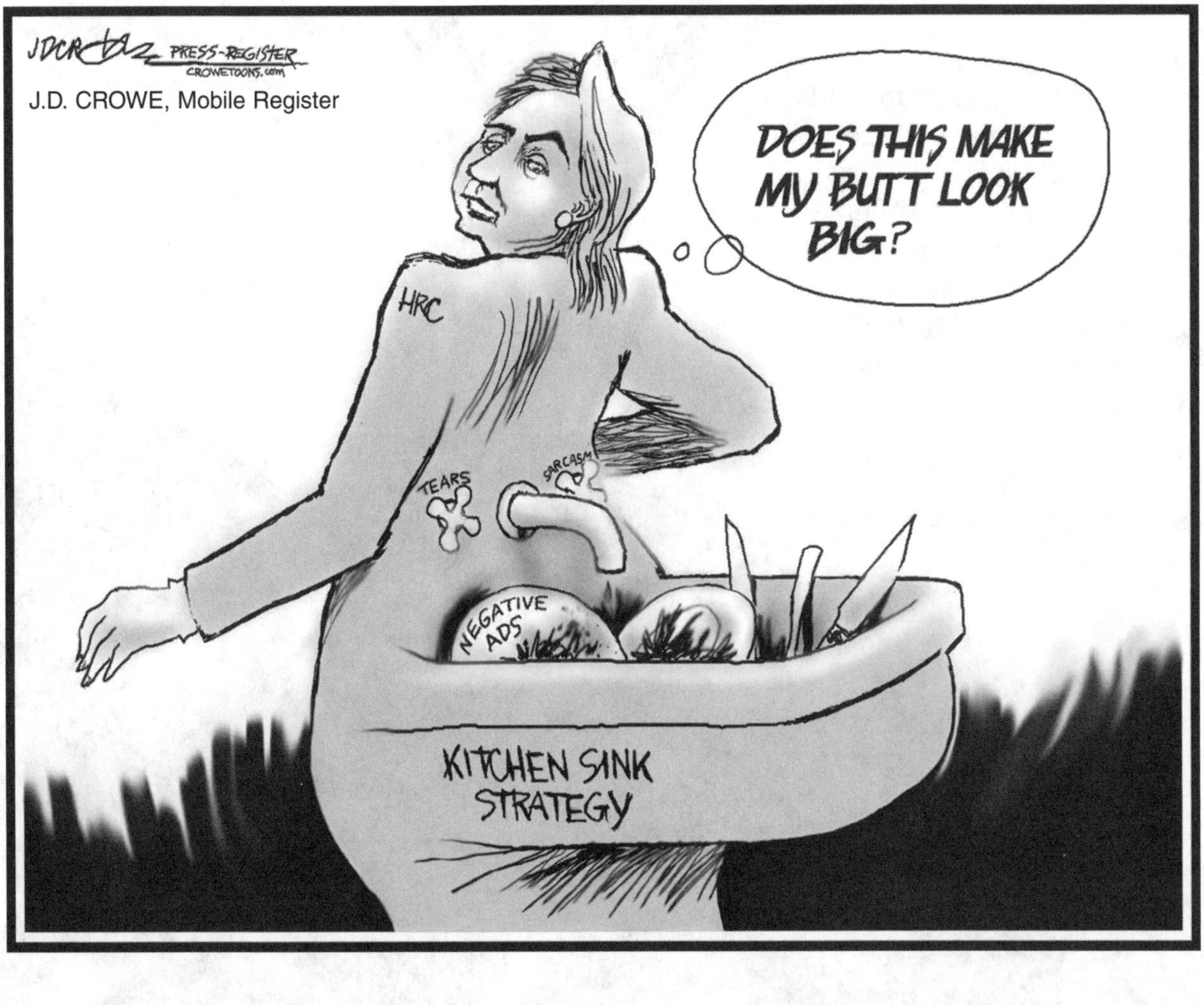

PRESS-REGISTER
CROWETOONS.com
DOES THIS MAKE MY BUTT LOOK BIG?
HRC
TEARS
SARCASM
NEGATIVE ADS
KITCHEN SINK STRATEGY

J.D. CROWE, Mobile Register

Barack Obama

DARIO CASTILLEJOS
Mexico

Barack Obama at first seemed like a long shot. He was the youngest and arguably most inexperienced, even in the early crowded field of candidates. But his charisma and megawatt smile lit a fire under the Democratic Party, and in the hearts of young liberal ladies across the country. At one point the raging Obamania seemed like it would carry the junior senator from Illinois straight through to the White House.

ERIC ALLIE, Politicalcartoons.com

GARY McCOY, Cagle Cartoons

JOE HELLER, Green Bay Press Gazette

OLLE JOHANSSON, Sweden

TAYLOR JONES
Politicalcartoons.com

MIKE KEEFE
Denver Post

J.D. CROWE, Mobile Register

JIMMY MARGULIES, The Record (NJ)

LARRY WRIGHT, Detroit News

M.e. COHEN, Politicalcartoons.com

BOB ENGLEHART, Hartford Courant

HE CAN'T WIN

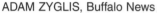

HE CAN'T GOVERN

HE CAN'T WIN A SECOND TERM

ERIC ALLIE, Politicalcartoons.com

ADAM ZYGLIS, Buffalo News

JOHN COLE, Scranton Times-Tribune

JOHN COLE, Scranton Times-Tribune

ADAM ZYGLIS, Buffalo News

SANDY HUFFAKER, Cagle Cartoons

GARY MCCOY, Cagle Cartoons

TAYLOR JONES
Politicalcartoons.com

Terry "Aislin" Mosher, Montreal Gazette

R.J. MATSON, St. Louis Post Dispatch

PAT BAGLEY, Salt Lake Tribune (UT)

WHY DID YOU DISAVOW YOUR PASTOR?

THE GOP WOULD HAVE USED HIM TO ATTACK ME!

AND WHY DID YOUR CAMPAIGN NOT ALLOW A MUSLIM WOMAN TO SIT BEHIND YOU?

WHOA! THERE'S A PHOTO THE GOP SMEAR MACHINE WOULD LOVE!

AND ABOUT YOUR BROKEN PROMISE TO ACCEPT PUBLIC CAMPAIGN FUNDS?

I HAD NO CHOICE! THE GOP WOULD HAVE SWIFT-BOATED ME!!

...AND "THE POLITICS OF HOPE?"

...NOW BLENDED WITH "THE PRACTICALITY OF PARANOIA."

JOHN COLE
Scranton
Times-Tribune

JOHN COLE
THE TIMES-TRIBUNE
SCRANTON, PA

DO YOU MIND?... YOU'RE IN MY SHOT!
Hillary '08

PAUL ZANETTI, Australia

"So your running mate list is a group of older white males?"

JIMMY MARGULIES, The Record (NJ)

I DIDN'T KNOW THE MESSIAH WORE THOSE KIND OF SANDALS

ERIC ALLIE
Politicalcartoons.com

JOHN TREVER, Albuquerque Journal

JOHN COLE, Scranton Times-Tribune

R.J. MATSON, St. Louis Post Dispatch

J.D. CROWE, Mobile Register

JOHN COLE, Scranton Times-Tribune

DAVID FITZSIMMONS, Arizona Daily Star

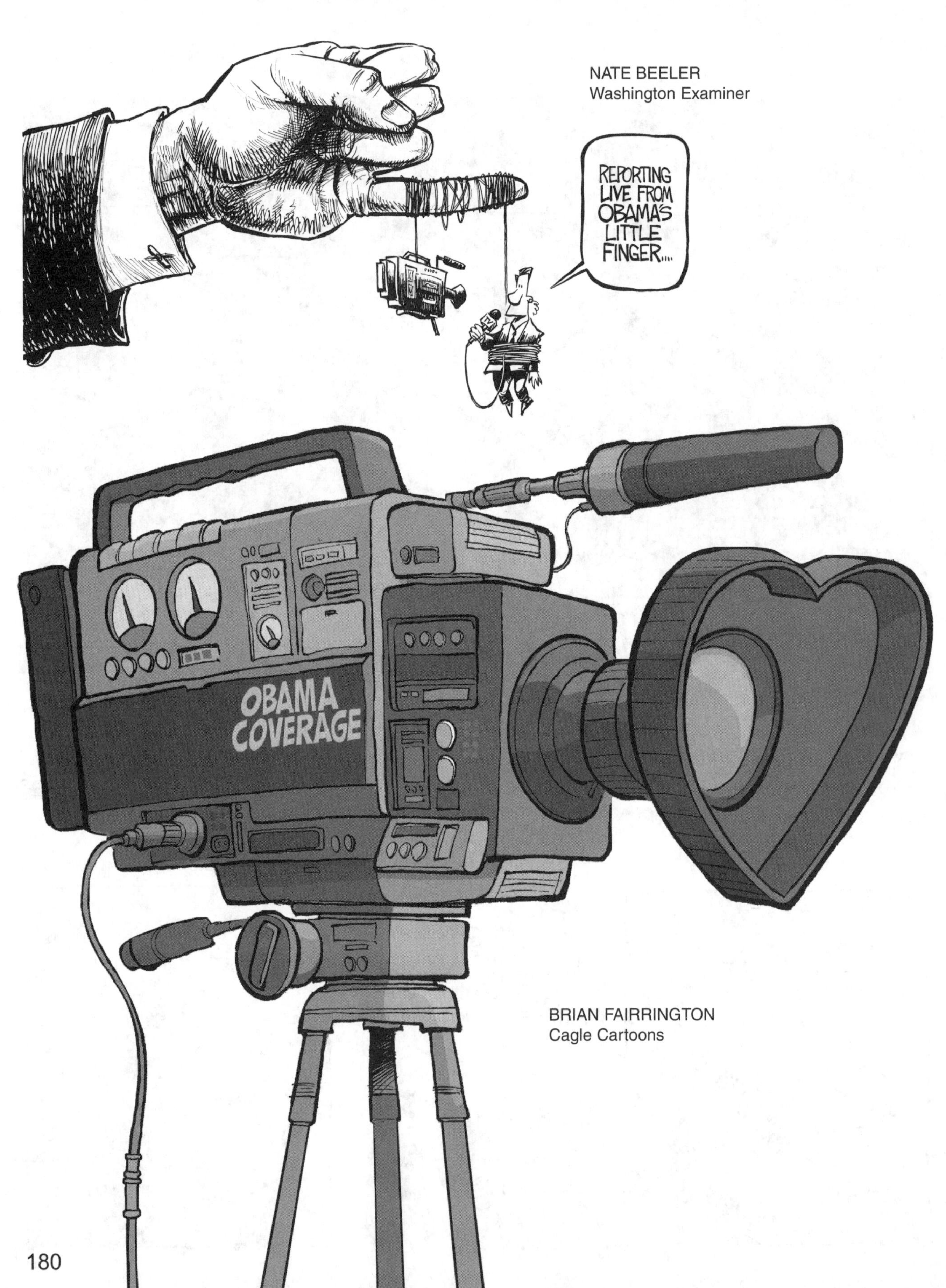
REPORTING LIVE FROM OBAMA'S LITTLE FINGER....
OBAMA COVERAGE

NATE BEELER
Washington Examiner

BRIAN FAIRRINGTON
Cagle Cartoons

NEWS ITEM: OBAMA COMPARED TO BRITNEY IN COMMERCIAL
=
BAGLEY
THE SALT LAKE TRIBUNE
I WILL FOLLOW HIM... FOLLOW HIM WHEREVER HE MAY GO...
AND NEAR HIM I ALWAYS WILL BE, FOR NOTHING CAN KEEP ME AWAY, HE IS MY DESTINY
I LOVE HIM, I LOVE HIM, I LOVE HIM, AND WHERE HE GOES I'LL FOLLOW, I'LL FOLLOW, I'LL FOLLOW, HE'LL ALWAYS BE MY TRUE LOVE...
MEDIA
I THINK WE SHOULD TRUST GEORGE W. BUSH IN EVERY DECISION HE MAKES AND SHOULD JUST SUPPORT THAT, YOU KNOW, AND BE FAITHFUL IN WHAT HAPPENS!*
* BRITNEY TO CNN SEPT. 2003
WHAT SHE SAID.
BRITNEY COMPARED TO McCAIN IN REAL LIFE
Q: IS THIS PERSON QUALIFIED TO BE THE NEXT PRESIDENT OF THE UNITED STATES?
A: MUST BE, I GUESS.
Mike Keefe THE DENVER POST 4-20-08

PAT BAGLEY, Salt Lake Tribune (UT)

RANDY BISH
Pittsburgh Tribune-Review

STEPHANE
PERAY
Thailand

MIKE KEEFE, Denver Post

RANDY BISH, Pittsburgh Tribune-Review

BOB ENGLEHART, Hartford Courant

DAVID FITZSIMMONS, Arizona Daily Star

J.D. CROWE, Mobile Register

PAT BAGLEY, Salt Lake Tribune (UT)

MICHAEL MCPARLANE, Politicalcartoons.com

ADAM ZYGLIS
Buffalo News

GARY MCCOY
Cagle Cartoons

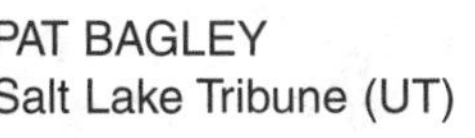

PAT BAGLEY
Salt Lake Tribune (UT)

YAAKOV KIRSCHEN, Jerusalem Post, Israel

JOHN DARKOW, Columbia Daily Tribune (MO)

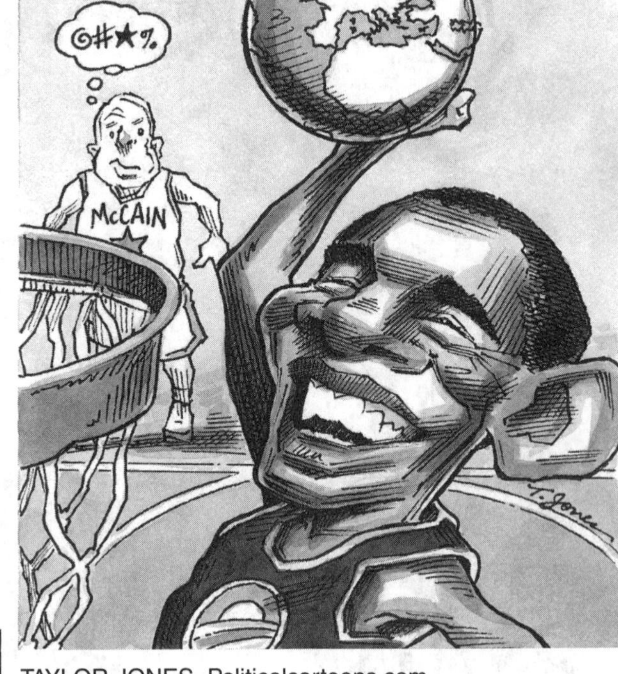

TAYLOR JONES, Politicalcartoons.com

MONTE WOLVERTON Cagle Cartoons

BOB ENGLEHART, Hartford Courant

I HAVE A NIGHTMARE...
News
PRESIDENT HILLARY CLINTON
mcparlane

MICHAEL MCPARLANE
Politicalcartoons.com

VOTE FOR THE PANTS YOU CAN BELIEVE IN

IAIN
GREEN
Scotland

R.J. MATSON
St. Louis Post Dispatch

★ ★ ★ THE FUTURE OF THE NATION WAS HANGING BY AL GORE

RECOUNT II

THE STORY OF THE LAST DEMOCRAT TO ENDORSE BARACK OBAMA

John McCain

Everyone had counted him out as an old, outlying coot, but John McCain came speeding from the back of the pack on his Straight-Talk Express to snatch the Republican nomination. But despite his late-game surge, McCain didn't quite appeal to the hard-nosed GOP base. The party that Bush led now saw the Arizona senator as a Republican in name only, with a long political history of economic conservatism, cracking down on big business and political pandering before he'd take up the pro-life cause.

But then, as if by magic, John McCain blossomed from a wormy moderate caterpillar into a conservative Republican butterfly -- just in time for campaign season. Unfortunately for him, cartoonists saw right through the emperor's new clothes.

MIKE LANE, Cagle Cartoons

MIKE KEEFE, Denver Post

JOHN COLE, Scranton Times-Tribune

DARYL CAGLE, MSNBC.com

PETAR PISMESTROVIC Austria

SANDY HUFFAKER, Cagle Cartoons

"BARACK OBAMA IS PROBABLY TOO YOUNG TO REMEMBER FULL SERVICE PANDERING."

R.J. MATSON, St. Louis Post Dispatch

And so it was that Midas was to touch his Golden Touch...

MIKE LANE, Cagle Cartoons

MIKE KEEFE, Denver Post

SANDY HUFFAKER, Cagle Cartoons

NATE BEELER, Washington Examiner

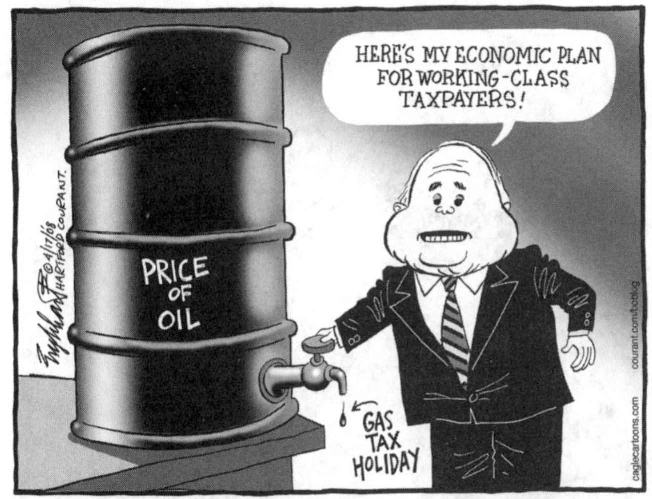

BOB ENGLEHART, Hartford Courant

"MY JOB IS TO CONVINCE VOTERS THIS IS STILL A GOOD LONG-TERM INVESTMENT..."

R.J. MATSON, Roll Call

MIKE KEEFE, Denver Post

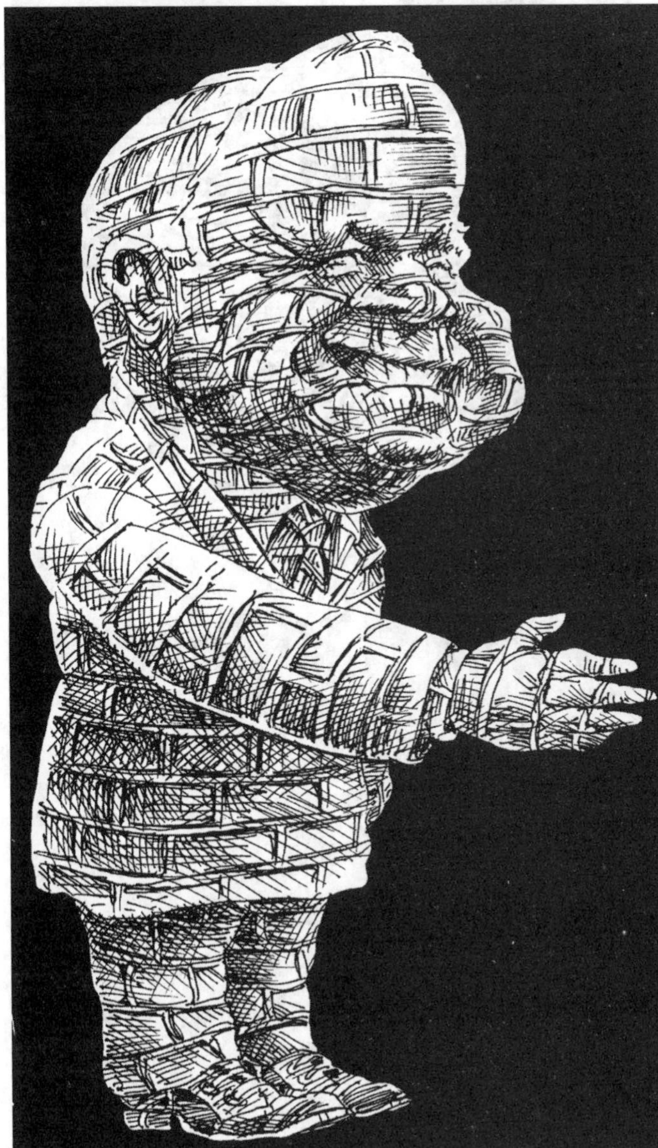

ANTONIO NERILICON, Mexico

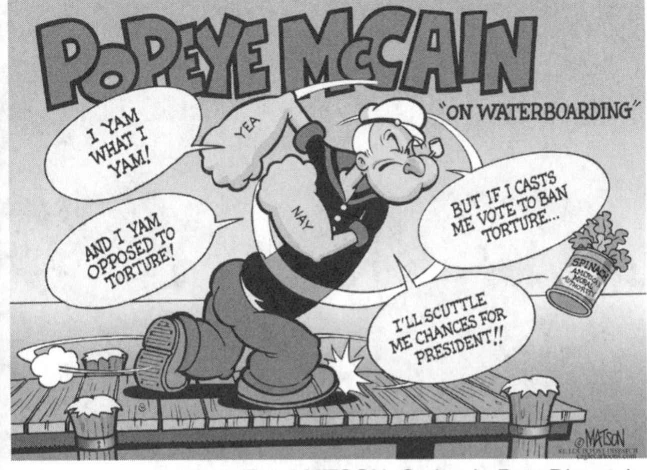

R.J. MATSON, St. Louis Post Dispatch

LAS VEGAS REVIEW · JOURNAL Jim Day '08

McCAIN NOMINATION

THE FAR RIGHT

A PARTY DIVIDED....

JIM DAY
Las Vegas
Review-Journal

JEFF PARKER, Florida Today

R.J. MATSON, Roll Call

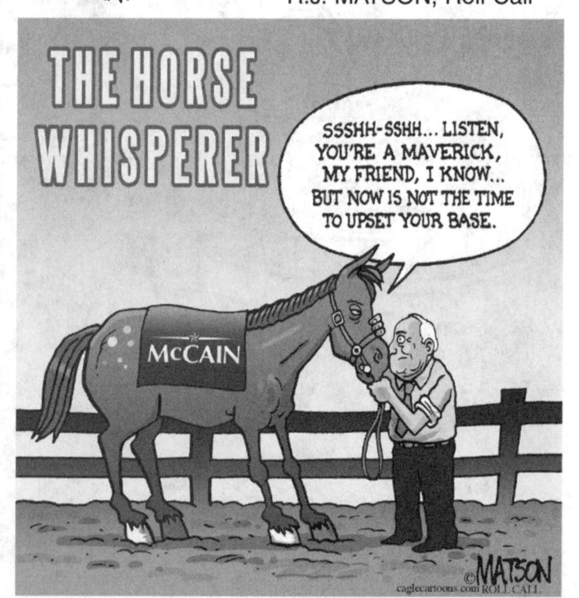

CAMERON CARDOW
Ottawa Citizen (Canada)

BUSH POLICIES
McCAIN

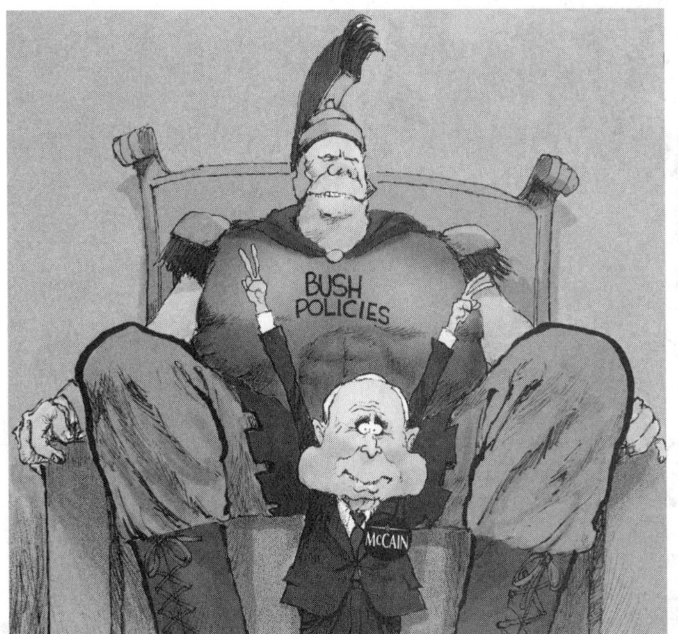

'FOUR MORE YEARS! FOUR MORE YEARS!'

PATRICK CHAPPATTE
International Herald Tribune

IT'S A HYBRID
Mc Cain
CONSERVATIVE
MODERATE
CHAPPATTE
Int'l Herald Tribune

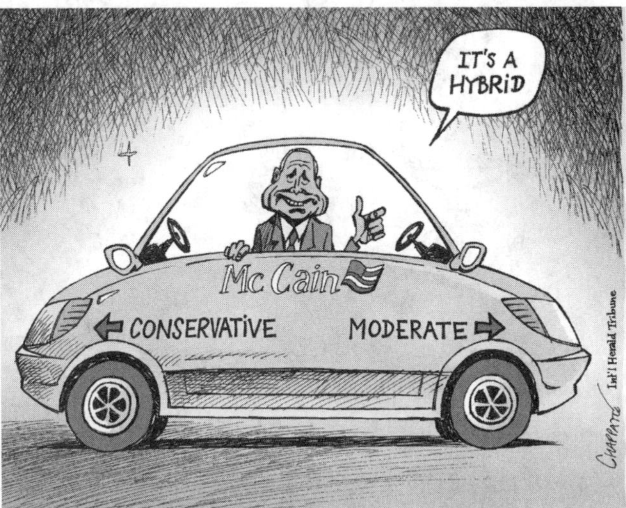

MONTE WOLVERTON, Cagle Cartoons

McCAIN ANGER MANAGEMENT SYSTEMS
CRANIAL STEAM TURBINE POWERED DYNAMO
BLOOD PRESSURE RELEASE VALVE
BULGING VEIN ATTENUATOR
FLUMMOX, FUMBLE AND FLOUNDER FILTER
RAMBLING INCOHERENCE STABILIZER
IRAN BOMBING RESTRAINER
F-WORD CANCELLATION DEVICE
ANEURISM BYPASS
DEFIBRILLATOR
FACIAL RUBEFACTION GOVERNOR
©2008 MONTE WOLVERTON
caglecartoons.com

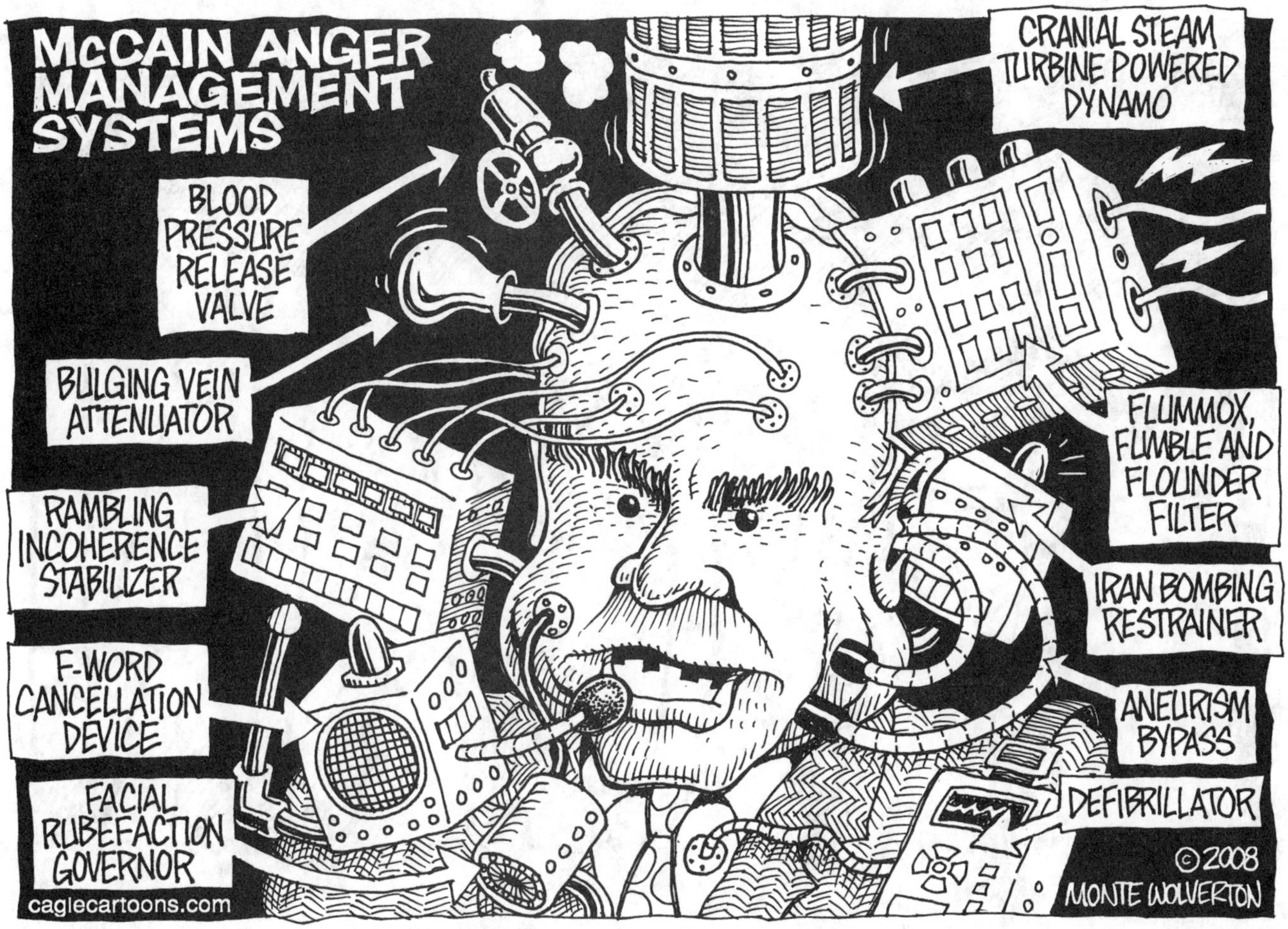

IRAQ
CRISIS
BUSH
JOHN MCCAIN
WE DON'T NEED ALL THE WEAPONS, AND AS PRESIDENT I'D BE PREPARED TO REDUCE OUR ARSENAL
LAUNCH
MCCAIN

ARCADIO ESQUIVEL
La Prensa, Panama

MICHAEL MCPARLANE, Politicalcartoons.com

JIM DAY, Las Vegas Review-Journal

MIKE LANE
Cagle Cartoons

JOHN TREVER, Albuquerque Journal

IAIN GREEN, Scotland

ADAM ZYGLIS, Buffalo News

JIM DAY, Las Vegas Review-Journal

GARY MCCOY, Cagle Cartoons

So JOHN, Despite our Differences, we'll TRY our Best to SUPPORT YOUR NOMINA-A-A-OH MY GOSH WHAT THE HELL IS GOING ON?!!!

JOHN DARKOW, Columbia Daily Tribune (MO)

BRIAN FAIRRINGTON, Cagle Cartoons

JOHN DARKOW, Columbia Daily Tribune (MO)

DAVID FITZSIMMONS
Arizona Daily Star

OLLE JOHANSSON
Sweden

DARIO CASTILLEJOS
Mexico

RANIER HACHFELD, Germany

Change for America

Amid growing dissatisfaction with President George W. Bush and the trajectory of America under his administration, Barack Obama embraced "change" as his semi-official '08 battle cry. Both Democrats and Republicans alike criticized Obama for overdoing the "change" rhetoric in his speeches, while candidates on both sides of the aisle co-opted his slogan for themselves. But in the end, Obama's supporters were the ones who really took the "change" to the polls in record numbers.

JOHN TREVER
Albuquerque Journal

BOB ENGLEHART, Hartford Courant

ERIC ALLIE, Cagle Cartoons

JOHN DARKOW, Columbia Daily Tribune (MO)

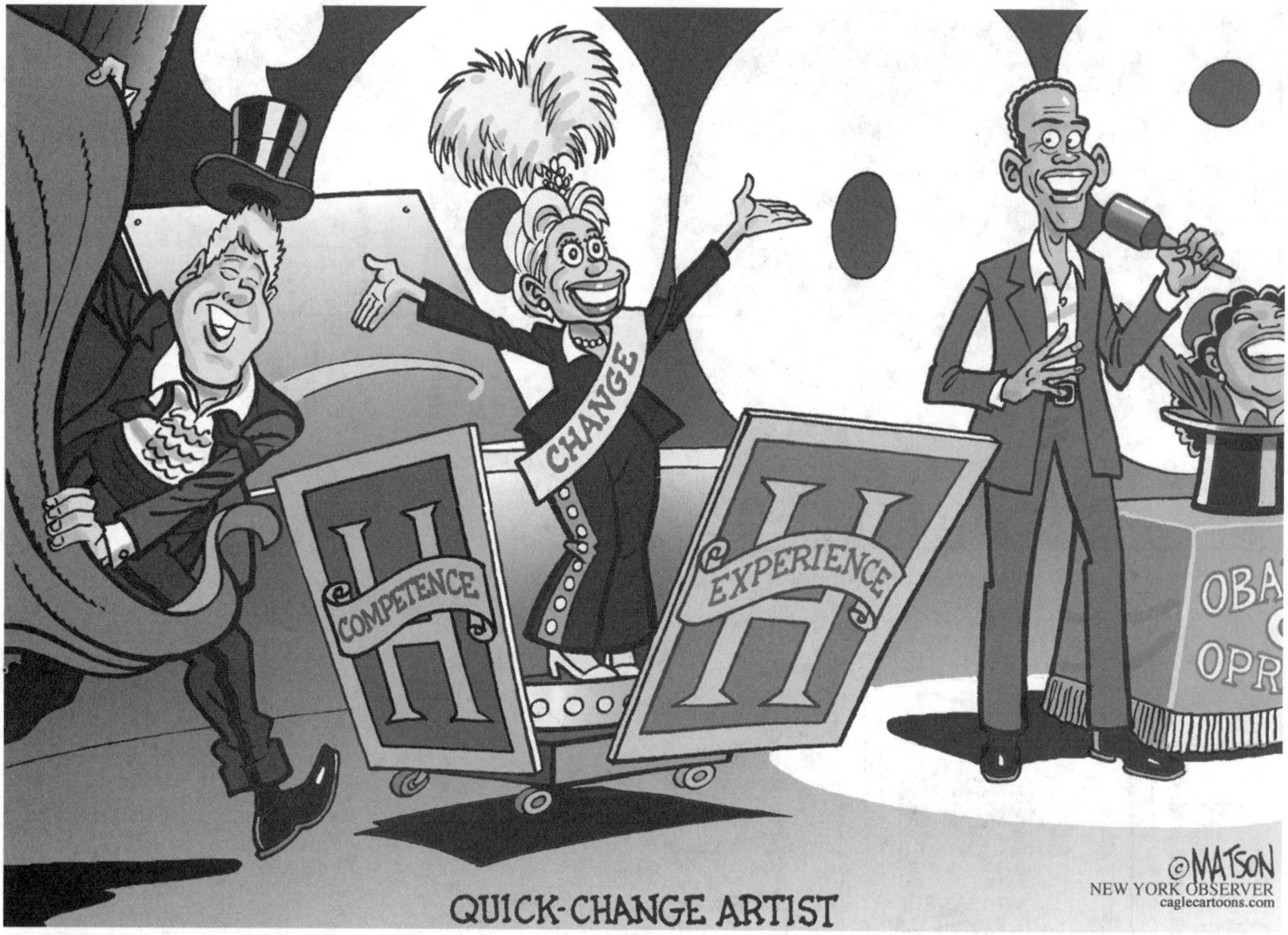

CHANGE
COMPETENCE
EXPERIENCE
OBA
OPR
QUICK-CHANGE ARTIST
©MATSON
NEW YORK OBSERVER
caglecartoons.com

R.J. MATSON, New York Observer

BEELER ©09 The Washington Examiner
CAGLECARTOONS.COM
WANT MY TWO CENTS ON THAT NO-GOOD, REAGAN-LOVER OBAMA?
BIIIIILLL...!
CHANGE

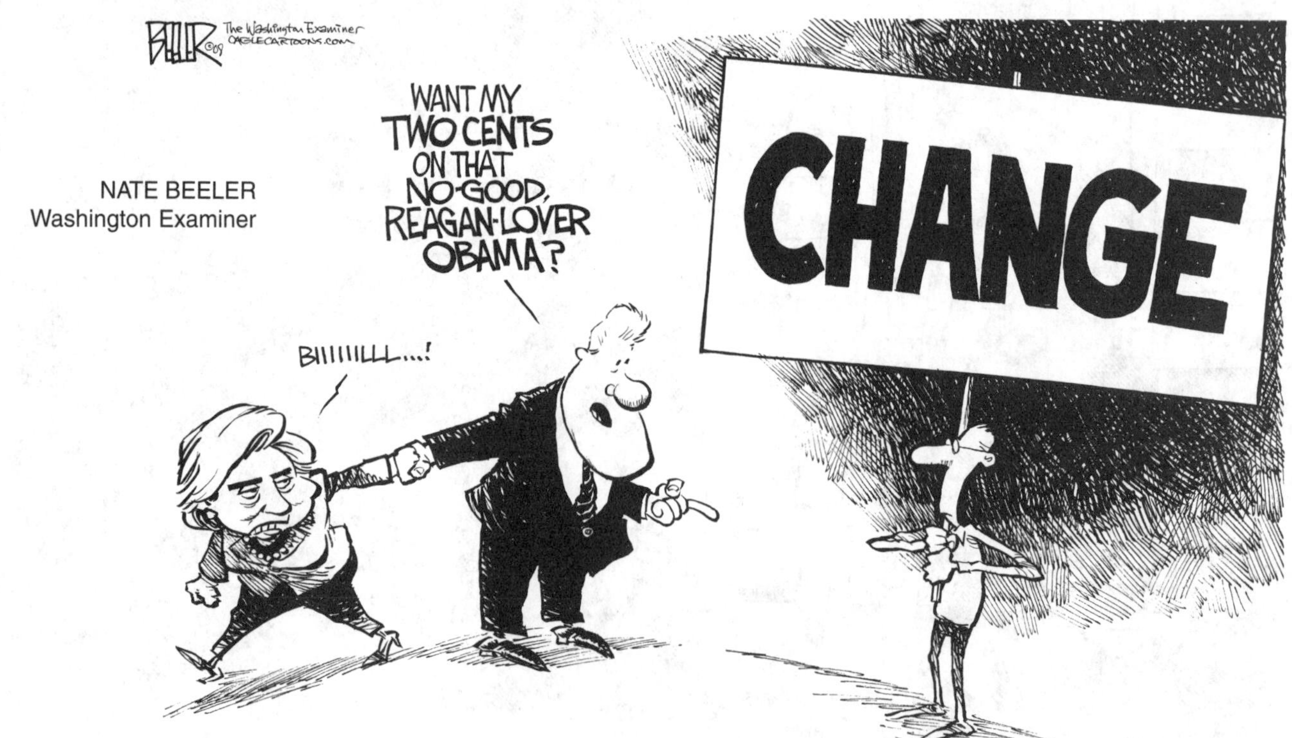

NATE BEELER
Washington Examiner

"CAN ANYONE BREAK A $100⁰⁰?"

R.J. MATSON
Roll Call

R.J. MATSON
St. Louis Post Dispatch

CHANGE

©MATSON ST. LOUIS POST-DISPATCH
caglecartoons.com

LARRY WRIGHT, Detroit News

JOHN COLE
Scranton Times-Tribune

FREDERICK DELIGNE
Nice-Matin, France

BRIAN FAIRRINGTON
Cagle Cartoons

ERIC ALLIE
Politicalcartoons.com

Hillary for V.P.

After conceding to Barack Obama and formally withdrawing from the presidential pack, Hillary mounted her second campaign of the season for the vice presidency. This one was a tad more subtle than Hillary's previous outing, but just about as successful. She seemed like an obvious running mate – the yin to Obama's yang. But Clinton had perhaps stepped on too many toes on her first heavy-footed romp down the presidential campaign trail to be a serious contender for Obama's second-in-command.

FREDERICK DELIGNE
Nice-Matin, France

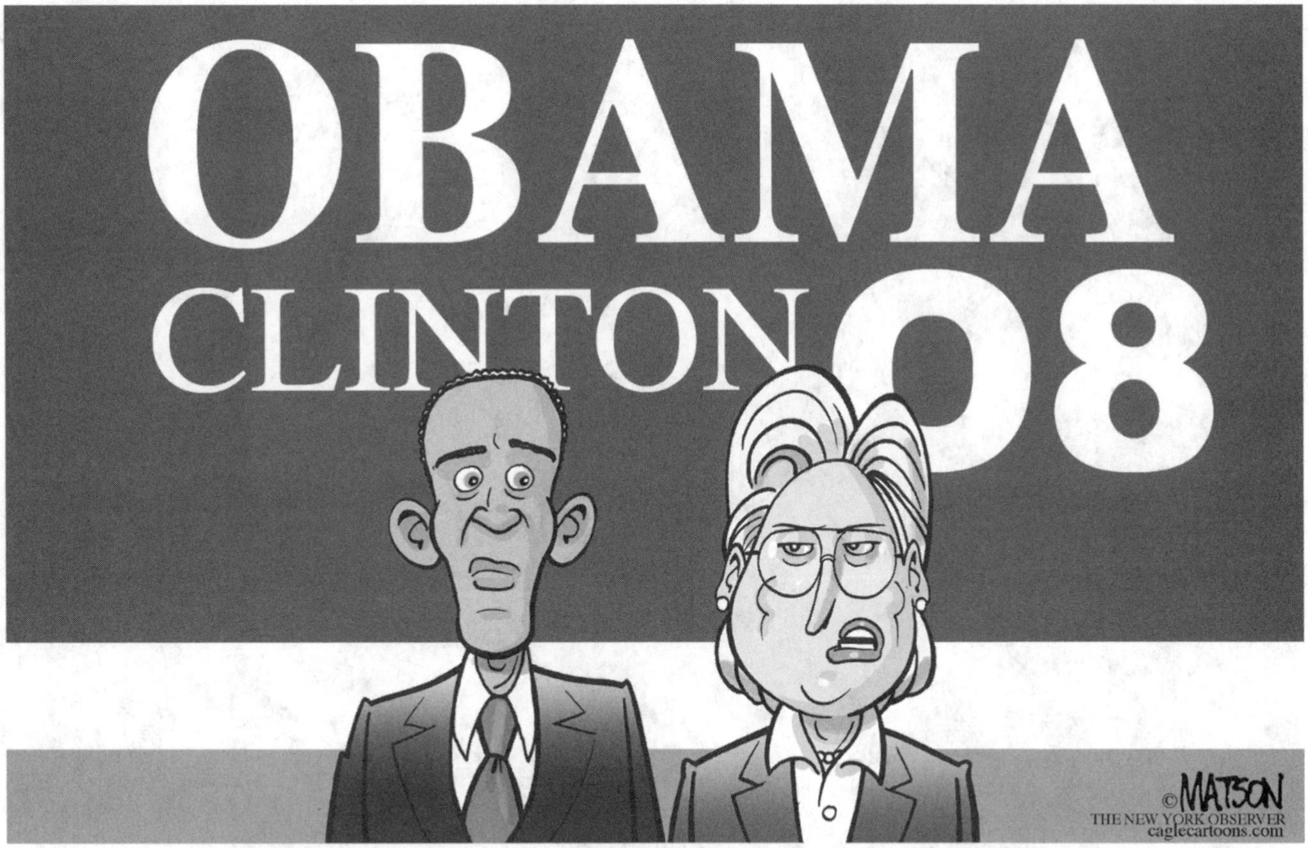

"HERE'S THE DEAL. YOU GET TO BE THE FIRST BLACK PRESIDENT, AND I GET TO BE THE FIRST WOMAN DICK CHENEY."

R.J. MATSON
New York Observer

AT LAST, WE'RE REUNITED!

STEP ON THE GAS!

LARRY WRIGHT
Detroit News

JOHN COLE, Scranton Times-Tribune

MIKE KEEFE
Denver Post

ADAM ZYGLIS
Buffalo News

R.J. MATSON, Roll Call

DARYL CAGLE
MSNBC.COM

PATRICK CHAPPATTE
International Herald Tribune

SANDY HUFFAKER
Cagle Cartoons

BOB
ENGLEHART
Hartford
Courant

JOHN DARKOW
Columbia Daily Tribune (MO)

JOHN TREVER
Albuquerque Journal

HILLARY FOR V.P.

NATE BEELER
Washington Examiner

JEFF PARKER
Florida Today

Obama vs. McCain

After many contentious months of primaries, micro-scandals, and media frenzy, Barack Obama and John McCain emerged from a wide field of candidates to take their parties' respective nominations. And although Hillary was certainly a favorite of cartoonists, the black-and-white, old-and-young, charismatic-and-boring dichotomy between Obama and McCain was a funnier target than any pantsuit in Clinton's closet.

TAYLOR JONES
Politicalcartoons.com

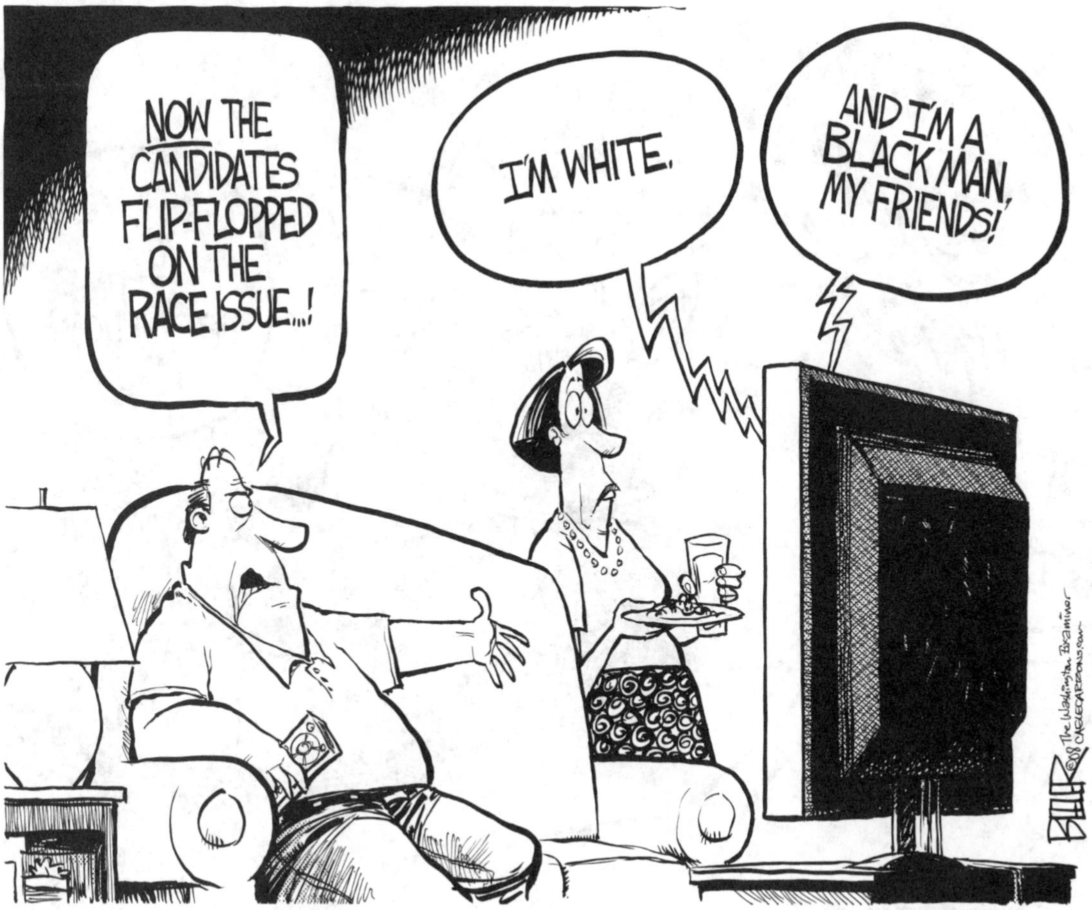

NOW THE CANDIDATES FLIP-FLOPPED ON THE RACE ISSUE...!

I'M WHITE.

AND I'M A BLACK MAN, MY FRIENDS!

NATE BEELER
Washington
Examiner

JIMMY MARGULIES
The Record (NJ)

INTER-NET

SCREEEEE

SQUAWW

GIVE ME THAT OLD TIME REPUBLICAN MUSIC

McC.

MIKE LANE
Cagle Cartoons

IAIN GREEN, Scotland

ADAM ZYGLIS, Buffalo News

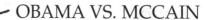

CHRISTO
KOMARNITSKI
Bulgaria

JOHN DARKOW
Columbia Daily
Tribune (MO)

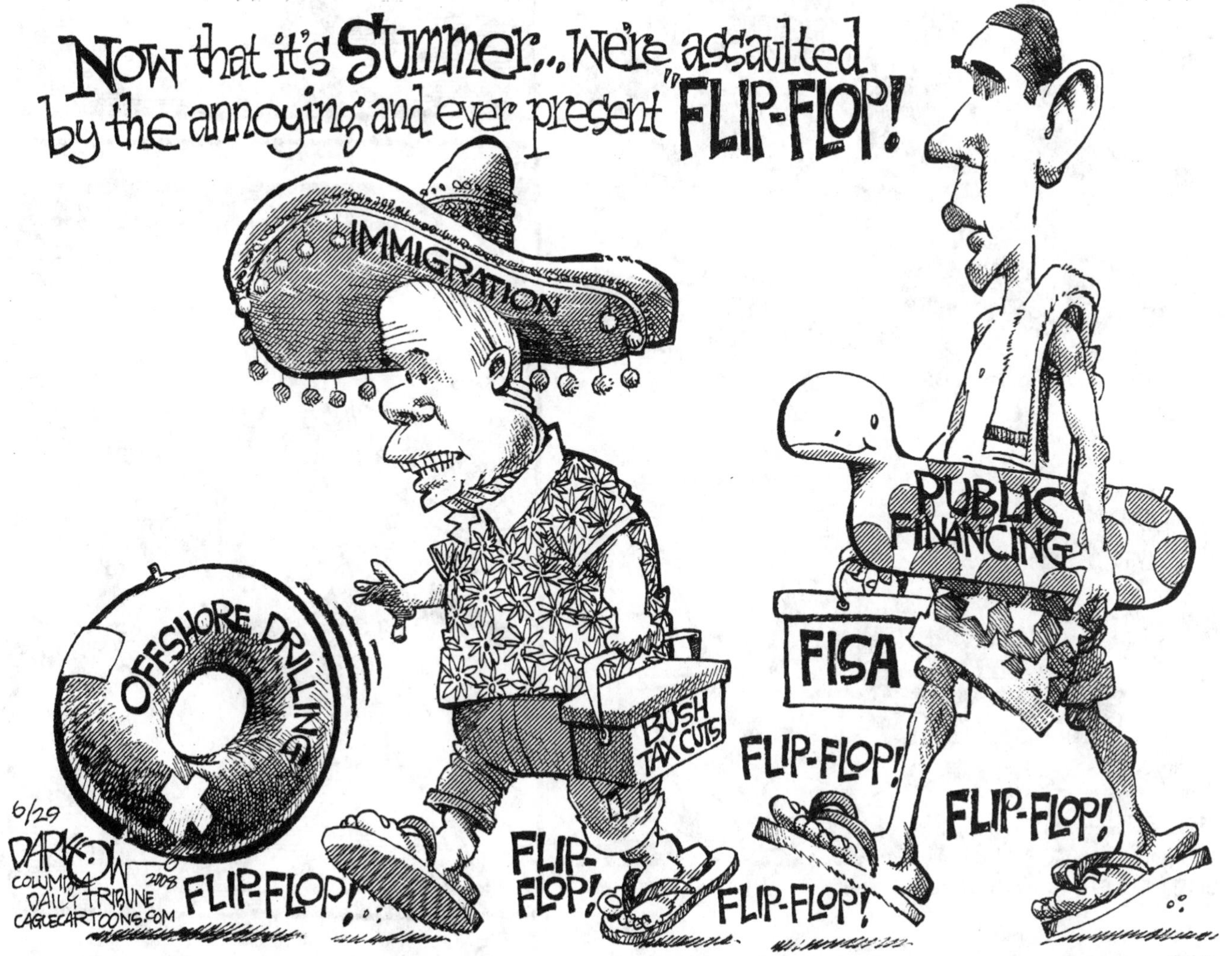

Now that it's Summer... we're assaulted by the annoying and ever present "FLIP-FLOP!"

IMMIGRATION

PUBLIC FINANCING

FISA

OFFSHORE DRILLING

BUSH TAX CUTS

FLIP-FLOP!

FLIP-FLOP!

FLIP-FLOP!

FLIP-FLOP!

FLIP-FLOP!

FLIP-FLOP!

6/29 DARKOW 2008 COLUMBIA DAILY TRIBUNE CAGLECARTOONS.COM

DAVID FITZSIMMONS, Arizona Daily Star

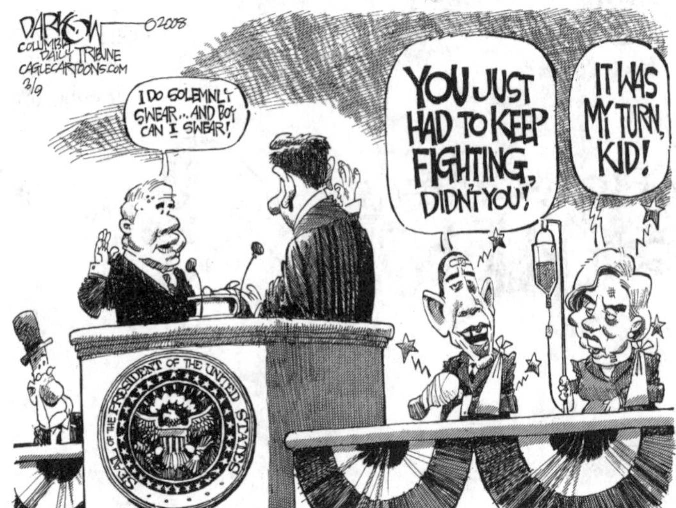

JOHN DARKOW, Columbia Daily Tribune (MO

JOE HELLER, Green Bay Press Gazette

BOB ENGLEHART Hartford Courant

PAT BAGLEY
Salt Lake Tribune (UT)

ERIC ALLIE
Politicalcartoons.com

MIKE KEEFE
Denver Post

JOE HELLER
Green Bay Press Gazette

DAVID FITZSIMMONS, Arizona Daily Star

CANDIDATES FAITH FORUM
LET'S SEE... WE'VE DONE OPRAH, JAY LENO, THE DALI LAMA JON STEWART and NOW RICK WARREN. WHEN DO WE DO THE POPE?
AFTER DEEPAK. AND BEFORE DR. PHIL.
DO UNTO OTHERS. THEN DENY YOUR CAMPAIGN HAD ANYTHING TO DO WITH IT.
FITZSIMMONS ©THE ARIZ DAILY STAR 2008

GOTTA CONVINCE THESE PEOPLE THAT I'M NOT A MUSLIM!
GOTTA CONVINCE THESE PEOPLE THAT I'M BIGGER THAN THE POPE!
GOTTA CONVINCE THESE PEOPLE THAT OBAMA'S A MUSLIM!
RICK WARREN
© 2008 MONTE WOLVERTON
caglecartoons.com

MONTE WOLVERTON
Cagle Cartoons

OBAMA AND McCAIN.

WHAT A PAIR OF FLIP-FLOPPERS.

ALWAYS FUDGING THEIR POSITIONS.

WAFFLING ON WHAT THEY BELIEVE.

THEY SHOULD TAKE A STAND AND STICK TO IT!

IGNORE THE VAGARIES OF A FICKLE PUBLIC!

STAND ATHWART THE WINDS OF POLITICAL FANCY!

STAY THE
ER.. COURSE... UM...

OK.
NEVER MIND.
JOHN COLE

JOHN COLE
Scranton
Times-Tribune

PARESH
MEXICO
OBAMA
McCAIN
NAFTA
Migration
ANTI-DRUG AID
HISPANIC-AMERICAN VOTERS
OUR FAVOURITE PUNCH BAG!

PARESH
NATH
India

LARRY WRIGHT
Detroit News

STARTING LINE
WHOOOOOOOOOOOOSH
OIL SPECULATORS
©2008 LARRY WRIGHT THE DETROIT NEWS

ANDY SINGER
No Exit

SINGER
IT'S HAWK MAN AND HIS "CROOKED LOGIC EXPRESS" VERSUS
•I OPPOSE TORTURE, UNLESS IT'S DONE BY A NON-MILITARY AGENCY LIKE THE C.I.A.
•I'LL REDUCE GLOBAL WARMING BY OFFSHORE DRILLING AND BURNING MORE OIL!
•I'LL CREATE PEACE AND SECURITY BY ATTACKING IRAN AND OCCUPYING IRAQ ...FOREVER!
•I'LL FIX THE ECONOMY BY DOING NOTHING AND CONTINUING G.W. BUSH'S FAILED POLICIES

CHAMELEON MAN—A WAFFLING COMPROMISER IN THE BILL CLINTON TRADITION
•I PLEDGED TO LIMIT MYSELF TO PUBLIC CAMPAIGN FINANCING BUT, WHEN I GOT CASH, I CHANGED MY MIND.
•I OPPOSED OFFSHORE OIL DRILLING ... BUT NOW I SUPPORT IT.
•I SUPPORT CIVIL LIBERTIES BUT I VOTED FOR A F.I.S.A. BILL THAT GREATLY CURTAILED THEM.
•I PROMISE TO BRING THE TROOPS HOME FROM IRAQ ... BUT NOT TOO FAST!

Democratic National Convention

The always star-studded Democratic National Convention/self-congratulatory rally/press conference convened on Denver, Colorado this year to rabble-rousing protests from flailing lefties and Hillary-supporters alike. Everyone was worried that Hillary Clinton would steal Barack Obama's spotlight after her narrow defeat just a few months earlier. But Hillary used her chunk of consolatory stage time to try to unite the party to the Obama cause. Good thing, too -- it may have salvaged her career in the Democratic party, and in the political cartoons.

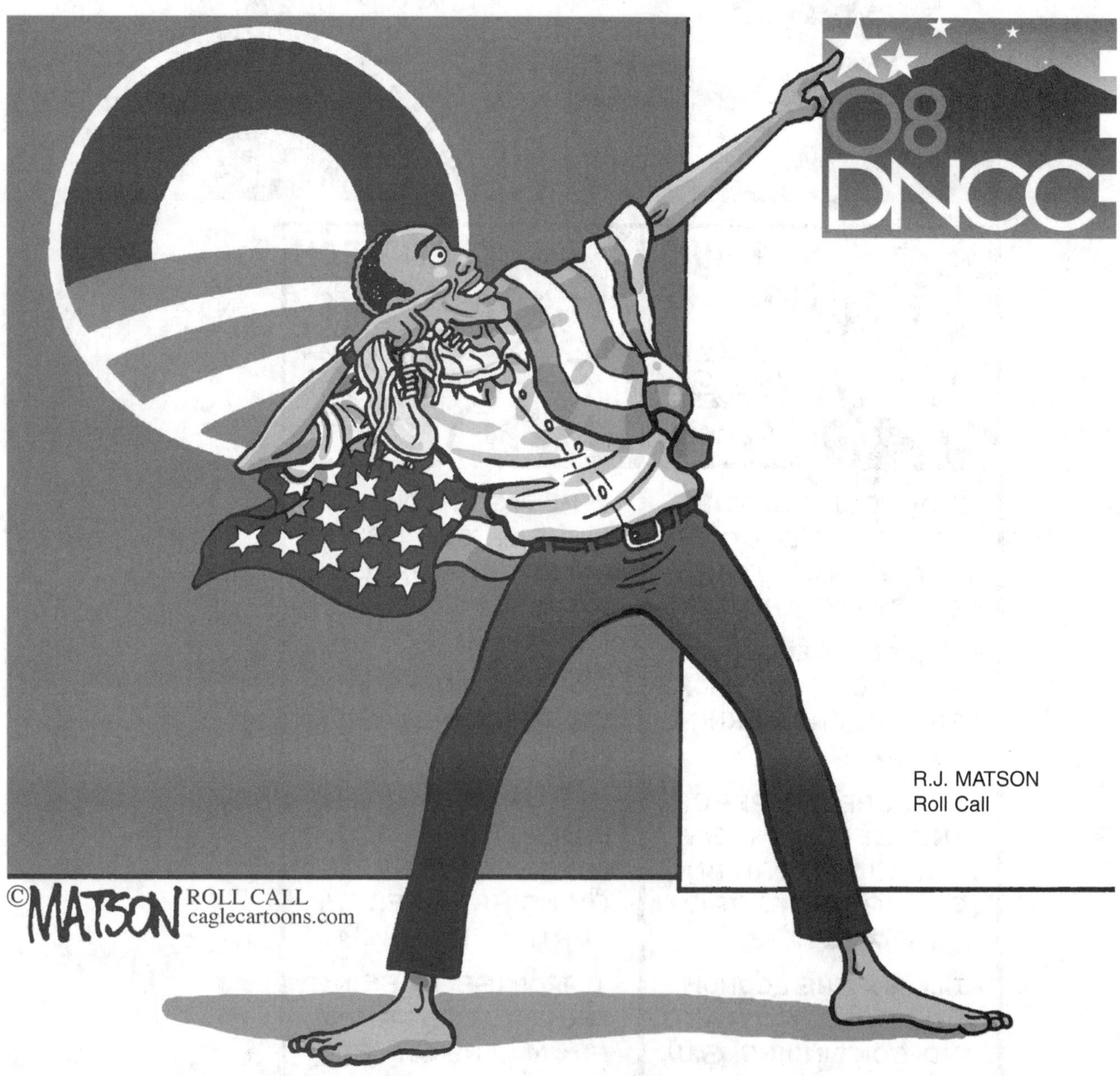
08
DNCC
R.J. MATSON
Roll Call
©MATSON ROLL CALL
caglecartoons.com
BARACK USAIN BOLT OBAMA

THE SECOND COMING

08 DNC

OBAMA

"OK, THIS IS TOO MUCH..."

CAM CARDOW, Ottawa Citizen

JIMMY MARGULIES, The Record (NJ)

JOE HELLER, Green Bay Press Gazette

As the FAITHFUL will LATER TELL IT:

The Heavens parted and Lo!
The Lord gaveth His Obama son,
and setteth him down uponeth
the 50-yard line....

CHANGE

UNITY

WE BELIEVE

OBAMA

HOPE

DNC

WE ♥ YOU, OBAMA

YES!

CHANGE NOW!

OBAMA

CHANGE

HOPE!

©'08 The Washington Examiner CAGLECARTOONS.COM

NATE BEELER, Washington Examiner

ADAM ZYGLIS, Buffalo News

RANIER HACHFELD, Germany

BEFORE YOU GO WALKIN' ON WATER, MOSES WANTS TO DO HER THING ONE LAST TIME...
NOMINEE
CONVENTION SCHEDULE
THE BLUE SEA
©2008 THE BUFFALO NEWS CAGLECARTOONS.COM
KENNEDY
BIDEN
Hillary
HACHFELD

YES WE CAN
OBAMA 2008
NO WE CAN'T
DEM 08
YOU'RE A HILLARY DELEGATE AREN'T YOU?
Hillary08
Official Democratic Jackass headgear
the Great Liberal Party Animal
Drinks wine, whines about Republicans
LOTS of HOT AIR
This Guy Knows how many houses he owns...one. (and it's in foreclosure)
see: "Taxpayer Bailout"
CHANGE
BIG GUY
OBAMA
TAX ME
08
Hug a Tree ABORT a baby
Time to trivialize the Holocaust by comparing Bush to Hitler again
Like his waistline, he wants Government to be big & bloated
Democratic anti-abstinence Kit (assorted flavored condoms ages 14 year and up)
DNC DENVER
Listens to Dixie Chicks on his IPOD

DAVID FITZSIMMONS, Arizona Daily Star

JIM DAY, Las Vegas Review Journal

BRIAN FAIRRINGTON, Cagle Cartoons

Biden's Bid for V.P.

Barack Obama shocked no one by not choosing Hillary Clinton to be his running mate -- though his pick of Joe Biden did come as something of a surprise. Biden's own bid for the White House took a nosedive after pundits jumped on his "clean, articulate and bright" remarks about Obama, but he had the years of experience, especially in foreign policy, to complement the Illinois senator.

Cartoonists were glad to have Biden's history of missteps (not to mention his hair plugs) on the ticket, but they were still sad to lose such a colorful character as Hillary.

TAYLOR JONES
Politicalcartoons.com

©Taylor Jones

ERIC ALLIE
Cagle Cartoons

DARYL CAGLE
MSNBC.COM

I FULLY ENDORSE THE DEVELOPMENT OF ALTERNATIVE ENERGY SOURCES LIKE SOLAR, BIOMASS, GEOTHERMAL..

FURTHERMORE
AND WHILE I'M ON THE SUBJECT..
BUT LET ME JUST ADD...
JOHN COLE
Scranton
Times-Tribune

TAYLOR JONES
Politicalcartoons.com

J.D. CROWE
Mobile Register

BARACK OBAMA DOESN'T LOOK LIKE ALL THOSE PRESIDENTS ON THE DOLLAR BILLS.
JOE BIDEN, ON THE OTHER HAND... GIVE HIM SOME HAIR EXTENSIONS, POOF IT OUT A LITTLE...

MIKE KEEFE, Denver Post

BARK BARK BARACK BARK

ARTICULATE AND BRIGHT AND CLEAN AND NICE-LOOKING WE CAN BELIEVE IN!

CHANGE WE CAN BELIEVE IN

BIDEN

WELL, HE'S NOT COMPLETELY OFF-MESSAGE...

OBAMA BIDEN 2008

NATE BEELER
Washington Examiner

DAVID FITZSIMMONS, Arizona Daily Star

CLEARLY HE NEEDS A VICE-PRESIDENT WHO IS WISER AND MORE EXPERIENCED THAN HE IS TO HELP RUN THE SHOW. PATHETIC ISN'T IT? JUST NOD.

Taylor Jones 2008
YES, WE CAN!
WHAT SENATOR OBAMA MEANS TO SAY, LADIES AND GENTLEMEN, IS THIS: AN AFFIRMATION. TO AFFIRM. TO CERTIFY, AS WITH A THUMBS-UP GESTURE, IF YOU WILL -- AND SUGGEST THAT WE, AS AMERICANS, EACH AND EVERY ONE OF US, FROM ALASKA TO DELAWARE (THE FIRST STATE. THE STATE WITH THE BEST COMMEMORATIVE QUARTER, IN MY HUMBLE OPINION), TO AFFIRM THAT WE ARE READY, WILLING AND ABLE, FROM THE SLAG HEAPS OF SCRANTON TO THE SAND DUNES OF REHOBOTH, TO DO WHAT NEEDS TO BE DONE, WHAT JOHN McCAIN BUSH WON'T DO, TO AHIEVE WHAT WE NEED TO AND MUST ACHIEVE IN THE TWENTY-FIRST CENTURY -- AND, QUITE FRANKLY, FOR MANY, MANY CENTURIES TO COME. CENTURIES, WE TRUST, THAT WILL BE FREE OF MY FRIEND JOHN BUSH McCAIN.
©Taylor Jones

TAYLOR JONES, Politicalcartoons.com

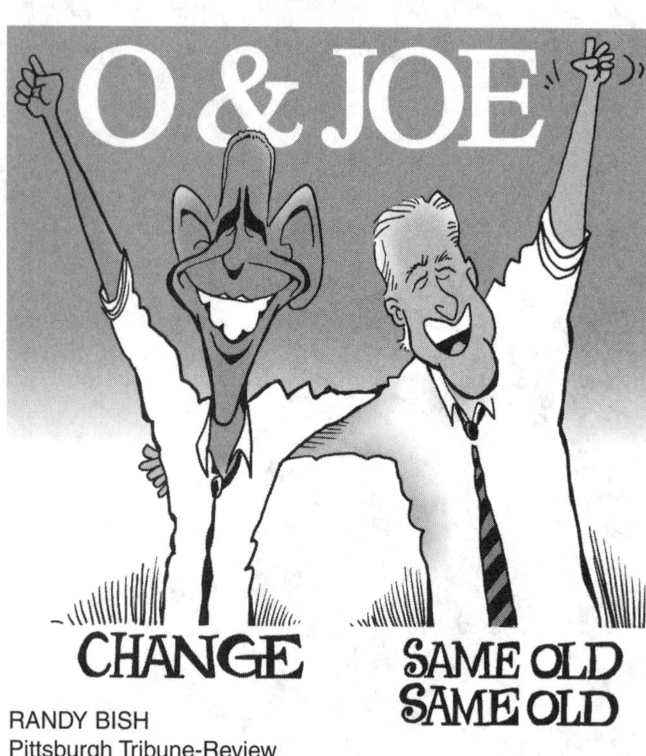

RANDY BISH
Pittsburgh Tribune-Review

I'M PSYCHED ABOUT BEING PICKED BY BARACK AS HIS RUNNING MATE!
AFTER ALL, HE'S THE FIRST MAINSTREAM AFRICAN-AMERICAN WHO IS ARTICULATE AND BRIGHT AND CLEAN...
BIDEN

GARY MCCOY, Cagle Cartoons

BIDEN

STEPHANE
PERAY
Thailand

STEPH

MONTE WOLVERTON, Cagle Cartoons

BARACK'S BOY BIDEN
BITES BUSH BUDDY

SIC'M, JOE

OW!

4 MORE YEARS

CHOMP!

© 2008 MONTE WOLVERTON

caglecartoons.com

Palin's Bid for V.P.

John McCain shocked Democrats and Republicans alike when he chose pretty, bespectacled, "hockey mom" Sarah Palin, the little-known Alaska Governor, as his running mate. Palin had a short political resume, with only two years as governor and a handful as a small-town mayor; but her aggressive state reforms impressed McCain's maverick sensibilities, and the idea that she might woo angry Hillary voters was a plus, even though he'd only met her once before.

Palin favored "abstinence only" sex education, which made for a sharp, visual contrast with her unwed, pregnant, teenage daughter who she brought on stage with her often. Republican operatives screamed that the media should leave pregnant daughter Bristol alone – which only encouraged the cartoonists draw even more cartoons on the subject.

PAT BAGLEY, Salt Lake Tribune

"SHE'S EVEN PRETTIER THAN ROMNEY."

PALIN

REPUBLICANS GET ROLLING

PATRICK CORRIGAN, Toronto Star

HILLARY
HILLARY
DARYL CAGLE MSNBC.com

DARYL CAGLE, MSNBC.COM

Community Chest
YOU HAVE WON
SECOND PRIZE
IN A
BEAUTY CONTEST
COLLECT VICE
PRESIDENCY
VICE PRESIDE
APOLOGIES TO HASBRO
DARYL CAGLE MSNBC.com

DARYL CAGLE, MSNBC.COM

R.J. MATSON
St. Louis
Post-Dispatch

DAVID
FITZSIMMONS
Arizona Star

RIBER HANSSON
Sweden

John McCain hoping that Bristol Palin's baby arrives before November 4th and that it is born glowing and wearing a beard and babbling in Aramaic about what a kick ass virgin its mother is.
MR.FISH

DWAYNE BOOTH, "Mr. Fish," L.A. Weekly

PETER NICHOLSON, Australia

JERRY SPRINGER
You know what happened to the moose, don't you Levi!
McCAIN
Who would've thought I'd be back covering National Affairs?!
4 Sept 08
Nicholson

J.D. CROWE
Mobile Press-Register

BRIAN FAIRRINGTON
Cagle Cartoons

McCain chose a woman for his V.P. running mate...

...normally we would report this story around-the-clock non-stop for weeks...but if we did that we couldn't devote all of our time to...

NEWS

FAIRRINGTON 09/08 CAGLECARTOONS

DON'T YOU WORRY, I'LL HAVE A PLUMBER OVER TO FIX YOUR LEAKY PIPES AS SOON AS POSSIBLE.. HECK, WITH SO MANY PROPERTIES AND RENTERS, IT'S HARD TO KEEP UP.

PSSST... THAT'S YOUR NEW RUNNING MATE, SARAH PALIN, SENATOR McCAIN...

CAM CARDOW
Ottawa Citizen

NATE BEELER
Washington Examiner

JOHN DARKOW
Columbia (MO) Daily Tribune

"...AND WHAT'S MORE, MY SOURCES TELL ME, THE PALIN FAMILY WILL SOON BE BLESSED WITH A *SECOND* SHOTGUN WEDDING!"

R.J. MATSON, New York Observer

CAMERON CARDOW
Ottawa Citizen (Canada)

NO CONDOMS IN SCHOOLS! NO SEX EDUCATION! ABSTINENCE ONLY!

I'M STRICTLY A PRIVATE MATTER.

DARYL CAGLE MSNBC.COM

DARYL CAGLE
MSNBC.COM

With regard to Sarah Palin's pregnant daughter...
McCAIN '08

NO ABORTION FOR ANY WOMAN. EVER

We expect everyone to respect the Palin family's privacy...
McCAIN '08
MARGULIES

JIMMY MARGULIES
The Record (NJ)

MIKE KEEFE
Denver Post

PATRICK CHAPPATTE
International Herald Tribune

FREDERICK DELIGNE
Nice-Matin, France

NATE BEELER
Washington Examiner

PAT BAGLEY
Salt Lake Tribune

THIS POOR LI'L GAL IS IN THE FIX SHE'S IN...
...BECAUSE OF YOU!
ME? BUT I DIDN'T DO ANYTHING
IT'S BECAUSE OF YOUR AMORAL DARWINISM and CONDOMS THAT THIS POOR GIRL IS IN A FAMILY WAY!
?!?
WATCH OUT FOR OL' BABY-KILLER HERE...
...FORE YA KNOW IT HE'LL GIVE YA AN ABORTION AND SOME SOB STORY 'BOUT POLAR BEARS...
THIS IS OUTRAGEOUS!
KILL... MY... BABY...?
NOW LOOK WHAT YOU GONE AND DONE-
UPSET THE LITTLE DEAR!

Republican National Convention

The Republican National Convention started as a washout when Hurricane Gustav hit New Orleans and reminded everyone of the Bush Administration's terrible response to Hurricane Katrina. The GOP favored discretion over hoopla and scaled the convention back as television news centered on storm coverage. Conservative pundits heaved a sigh of relief when unpopular President Bush announced that he would not visit the convention.

DARYL CAGLE
MSNBC.com

J.D. CROWE
Moblie Press-Register

FREDERICK DELIGNE
Nice, France

PATRICK CHAPPATTE, International Herald Tribune

Artists Index